TRACKS
AND
TRACKING

TRACKS
AND
TRACKING
The Classic Guide to Seeing and Reading Animal Signs

Josef Brunner

Skyhorse Publishing

First published in 1923
First Skyhorse Publishing Edition 2014

Skyhorse Publishing books may be purchased in bulk at special discounts for sales promotion, corporate gifts, fund-raising, or educational purposes. Special editions can also be created to specifications. For details, contact the Special Sales Department, Skyhorse Publishing, 307 West 36th Street, 11th Floor, New York, NY 10018 or info@skyhorsepublishing.com.

www.skyhorsepublishing.com

10 9 8 7 6 5 4 3 2 1

Library of Congress Cataloging-in-Publication Data is available on file.

Cover design by Jane Sheppard
Cover photo credit: Thinkstock

Print ISBN: 978-1-62914-458-0
Ebook ISBN: 978-1-63220-152-2

Printed in the United States of America

CONTENTS

vii

CONTENTS

FOREWORD

TO derive the greatest pleasure from the pursuit of game, either large or small, it is necessary that the disciple of Nimrod be versed in the science of interpreting the meaning of tracks and trails. Nature is as an open book to the man who can read the signs of the woods and plains correctly; and where the uninitiated see only meaningless tracks, experienced hunters find them in many instances the guide to exhilarating sport and a desired trophy. To the tyro the finest tracking snow is useless and the marks he sees everywhere around him simply bewilder him. Were he able to read them as every hunter should, his day's sport would mean enjoyment and success, instead of disappointment and failure.

Game is not so plentiful as it used to be, and for this reason it is generally a waste of time—from the standpoint of the game bag—merely to tramp through the woods and trust to luck.

Moreover, the high-power, small-caliber rifles, which are so extensively used, very often lead to shots at distances at which it is not possible to place an immediately fatal bullet. This makes it the more necessary for the hunter to be able to read the signs correctly and to interpret aright the language of the trails. Every sportsman should consider it a sacred duty to bring to bay any animal he has wounded, and he should also regard it a matter of honor to acquire a working knowledge of tracks, trails, and signs. Then he will not, through ignorance, make carrion or wolf-bait of a noble creature which, in all reason, he should have secured.

A sportsman who is unable to interpret the meaning of tracks he encounters, however much game he may have killed by chance, luck, or with the assistance of others, will be considered a tyro in woodcraft by companions who have learned their lessons in this art.

Lack of opportunity on the part of the majority of sportsmen to become versed in tracking lore by actual experience, as well as the incompetence of a great number of guides, is the reason for this book. The contents represent the experience gained from twenty years of uninterrupted life in the great outdoors; and while only half of that time was spent in the pursuit and study of American game, the foreign experience was a considerable aid in arriving at definite conclusions, for the same species, with but few exceptions, show the same features in their trails the world over.

No space has been given to microscopic intricacies, since in the woods plain tracking lore is intricate enough. In practice whoever looks for exaggerated, fine, distinctive features in tracks and trails soon sees things which a sober-minded expert recognizes as imaginative.

*   *   *   *   *

It is generally understood that a track means the imprint left on the ground or snow by a passing creature. From its form and appearance the initiated are usually able to tell the species, and in some cases the variety, of animal that made it. Where the latter is not possible, a succession of tracks—the trail, in short—is almost invariably the means of reaching a proper decision. The expert considers not only tracks and trails, but also the " signs," among which are the behavior of animals under certain circumstances, blazed trees, bear logs, beaver stumps and cuttings, excrements, etc., etc. A mere treatise of tracks, trails and signs would in many instances leave the inexperienced man without a comprehensive knowledge; therefore certain actions of the hunted, and notes on hunting methods which have proved practical, although they are not generally known, have been introduced into the text.

It is believed that a thorough study of this book, including the illustrations, will enable the reader to become as well versed in tracking lore as he could by years of actual experience in the woods.

TRACKS AND TRACKING

TRACKS AND TRACKING

GENERAL REMARKS

About the Motive Features of Different Animals

TAKING it for granted that the arrangement of the individual tracks in the trail is due to the general anatomic make-up of the animal which made them, we have to consider four groups in the treatise on mammals.

The *first,* the members of which possess a length of body correctly proportional to their height, includes the deer, ox, bear, dog, and cat families.

The *second* includes rabbits, squirrels, and animals whose hind legs are very long in proportion to their front legs.

The *third* is made up of those animals whose legs, considering the length of their bodies, are very short—marten, mink, etc.

3

The *fourth* group embraces the animals whose legs are very short in proportion to the length of the body, and whose bodies, in addition to this, are disproportionately thick—beaver, badger, etc.

Of the various movements, we have to consider the walk, the trot, and the gallop. Animals of the first group plant the feet diagonally in the walk and trot. The hind foot track covers the one made by the forefoot of the same side. If the right forefoot touches the ground first, the left hind foot is placed next, then the left forefoot, and last the right hind foot. Thus four footfalls may be heard when hoofed animals are walking.

In the trot, which is but a hastened walk, the trail assumes more the form of a straight line, because the animal endeavors to plant the feet more under the middle of the body to obviate the swaying motion; and because of the quicker action, in which two feet touch the ground at the same moment, but two distinct footfalls can be heard.

The gallop, the quickest movement onward, is

4

a series of leaps or jumps. In it the hind feet serve mainly as propellers while the forefeet support and brace the body; and for this reason the former are placed side by side, or nearly so, while the latter stand one behind the other in the trail. The faster the gallop, the more closely do the tracks conform to these conditions. In the greatest speed of some members of the deer family the hind feet also come nearer the center line, as shown in the illustrations. As, by the velocity of the movement, the hind feet are thrown past the point where the forefeet strike the ground, their imprints appear in front of those of the latter, a fact which should be kept constantly in mind by the trailer, since, in the case of an animal with a broken leg, the appearance of the leap imprints are usually the only means to decide which leg is broken. In animals of the first group a broken foreleg is always more serious than an injured hind leg, and therefore the game is easier brought to bag.

In members of the second group there is but one motion, no matter whether they are moving slow or fast—the hind feet are always thrown

ahead of the forefeet, and the track picture is
that of the leap.

As the hind feet of animals of this group are
considerably larger than the forefeet, it is easily
determined which individual foot has made a
given track.

The animals of the third group move usually in
leaps, but on account of the length of body and
the shortness of the limbs, the hind feet are not
placed as far ahead of the front pair as in the
preceding group. At the usual gait the hind
feet cover the forefeet tracks, and the trail picture therefore shows a pair of tracks side by side
at regular distances. At a faster pace the trail
picture changes, as shown in the illustrations;
however, this is so seldom done as to be of almost
no consequence to the tracker.

Members of the fourth group, like those of the
first, walk and leap; however, the size of the body
and the shortness of the legs combine to make a
track picture entirely different from and not
easily confounded with the trail of the latter.
The individual tracks are close together, considering their size, and the toes of the hind feet almost

invariably point inward to a marked degree, reaching an extreme limit in the beaver and the badger.

With the exception of the members of the second group and the beaver, the hind feet of all animals are smaller than the forefeet, a fact which, in some instances, has its uses when following the trail

THE WHITE-TAILED OR VIRGINIA DEER

THOUGH the American sportsman still can enjoy in some districts, as an inheritance from prehistoric times, the pursuit of the majestic moose, and though the lordly elk still awakens the echoes in many of our mountain ranges with his challenging call, the game in which the great majority of hunters are pre-eminently interested is the elusive white-tailed deer, which is found in all the states except California, Nevada, Oregon, and Delaware, and because to bring it down demands, to say the least, no less skill than is required in the pursuit of its larger relatives.

Though, under ordinary conditions, a single track of any other animal is nearly sufficient to ascertain the species or variety, the case is different where white-tailed and mule deer are concerned—that is, if they inhabit the same locality; and even a small elk track may be taken for that of the white-tailed deer.

The track of a mule deer, roaming in rocky hills or out in the arid breaks of the Bad Lands, is of course a very different thing from that of a white-tail, but let the animals make their permanent stand in white-tail country proper, and almost all difference in their track soon disappears. It is evident that the sole of their hoof undergoes the same change as that of a horse, which can be ridden daily without shoes in dry regions, but which will get footsore within a day or two if it is transferred into a district where rain and dew moisten the grass and keep the ground damp.

Considering the individual track, the hoof of the Virginia deer evidently spreads easier than that of any other member of the family, except moose and caribou. It is because of this that, during the season when they are in good condition and in hunting time, the ridge of dirt or snow that is made between the two halves of the hoof, and left in the track, is much more conspicuous than that left by any other deer. However, if the conditions are not ideal—and they most certainly are not if snow is on the ground,

VIRGINIA DEER

under which circumstances most tracking is done—the variance appears so slight that it can be noticed only by examining minutely a perfect track, which may be found along the trail under some tree where not more than an inch of snow has fallen or at a barren spot.

The writer does not depend on the size of the track in deciding whether it was made by a buck or a doe, as he has seen many does which have made as large tracks as the largest bucks; and the common claim that rounded toes always indicate a buck he has also found to be a fallacy. Sometimes it is noticeable in the trail that the hind feet lag, *i. e.*, they do not quite reach the forefeet tracks. This almost invariably means an old buck which has become rather stiff with age. The chance that the same mark is made by an old sterile doe is remote, though, according to observations, possible.

Not infrequently, at least much oftener than with black-tail and elk, a marked difference between the two halves of the hoof may be observed in the track of the Virginia deer, and the tracks of the latter appear more slender than

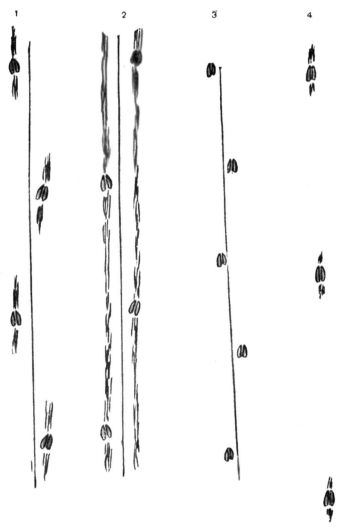

TRACKS OF VIRGINIA DEER

(1) Trail of buck before and after rutting season. (2) During rutting season the drag extends from one step to the next. (3) Trail of doe and fawn; the latter, however, takes still shorter steps. (4) Buck or doe trotting.

those of the former—that is, in the same locality. Some claim that they can always distinguish the track of Virginia from that of other deer, but the writer counts himself among those who can not, and he has noticed that the hunters who claim the skill are in the same predicament when out in the woods.

Accurate measurements with the divider and tapeline would possibly show some slight differences in the tracks of the various kinds of similar sized deer, but they would be so diminutive and variable as to be worthless in practice.

The trail, together with other signs, is much more significant of the doings, ailments and sex of the animal than an individual track would be. During the summer months the buck, and, it must be admitted, the sterile doe also, accumulates a considerable amount of fat; and the result is markedly shown in the placing of the feet, their tracks being an appreciable degree off the center line supposed to be under the middle of the body. For this reason the toes of the hoof point more outward than is usual in the doe and fawn. From this it might appear that a

16

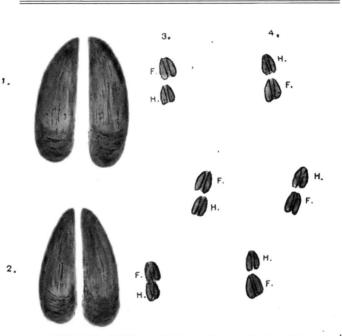

VIRGINIA DEER. (ONE-HALF NATURAL SIZE)

(1) Front track. (2) Hind track. (3) Lagging back of hind feet; sign of the old buck. (4) Overhastening; the sign of the young buck. 3 and 4 also apply to the elk bull.

single track, or a few of them, would be sufficient to decide the sex, but it is not; because any deer in crossing a trackable spot is likely to look to the right and then to the left, and the tracks will point in the direction the animal has looked.

Does heavy with fawns show similar features in their trail, but as there are no such does dur-

17

ing autumn, we can pass them over. A buck always has the tendency to drag his legs, a feature which reaches the climax during rutting season, while any doe, even the sterile, steps clean if the snow is less than one foot deep. This fact makes it possible to tell a buck's track with certainty, even if tracking conditions are not favorable, because there is always some displacement behind and in front of the tracks which is readily observed in sand or dry snow.

There is one other feature by which the trail of a white-tail buck can be distinguished from that of a doe, and even that of the buck of blacktails, and that is the animal's habit of scanning the surroundings while standing near trees, windfalls, and the like. An old buck at leisure will take careful observations two or three times inside of a hundred yards, except during the rutting season, when he is too busy to spend so much time for safety's sake, and he always does this from what he evidently considers cover.

In open forests are often seen places where the ground has been pawed up, and the ground covering, moss, leaves or sod, thrown in every direc-

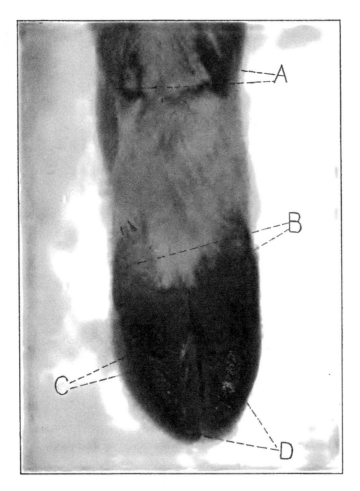

HIND FOOT OF VIRGINIA DEER. (SLIGHTLY REDUCED)
(A) Dew claws.   (B) Heels.   (C) Soles.   (D) Toes.

tion. This always indicates the presence of at
least two old bucks in the same locality, and is
never done by does.

About the first of September bucks begin to
cleanse their horns of the velvet and small trees
and bushes exhibit the signs of having been used
for that purpose. Where such signs are found
in roomy forests near dense thickets, the sportsman can, with moderate certainty, count on getting a trophy by stalking quietly or waiting from
sunrise to about 8 o'clock A.M., or from an hour
or so before sundown until dark. Of course it
is easier to get meat for the pot near streams and
feeding places, where there are plenty of tracks,
but as doe and fawn shooting aims at the base
of life, and as old bucks usually do not make
their appearance there as long as it is light enough
for a rifle shot, I would not advise one to stalk
or wait there at all. Stalking during rainy days
in open forests where bucks have left evidences,
such as blazed trees, will, as a rule, be rewarded.
At that time, game being comparatively undis-
turbed, most deer are shot at while standing, and
even a poor shot can hardly miss. However, as

tracking is more difficult than when snow covers the ground, it is advisable to watch the deer closely for the signs at the moment of firing.

The most important sign to observe is the action of the game when it receives the missile, since it is an evidence of where it was hit. If struck somewhere in the front half, it usually jumps into the air—that is, if it does not drop instantly, which incident we have no need to consider in this connection—and if struck in the hind half, it will kick out with the hind legs. A deer shot through the heart seldom drops immediately. After the first jump, which is often hardly perceptible and no doubt overlooked by the average hunter, it generally makes off at top speed, running close down to the ground. It may run only fifty yards, and it may run five hundred, but one thing is certain —the hunter can follow at once, and the animal will be dead by the time he reaches it.

The most striking exception to the rule of heart shots the writer saw in the Snowy Mountains, Montana, during 1904. A buck was galloping, broadside exposed, at a distance of about one hundred and twenty yards, and was fired at.

Four or five jumps after the shot was fired he stopped behind some trees, which prevented another shot. He remained hidden a few seconds, then trotted about thirty yards and stopped again; finally he trotted off, directly away from me, and if ever I would have sworn that a deer was missed, I would have done so then.

However, force of habit compelled me to follow the trail, and about two hundred yards from where he stopped last, the buck lay stone dead. The bullet, a steel-jacketed .30 U. S., had penetrated the heart squarely, and made a hole the size of a quarter. There was not a drop of blood along the trail. Moral: Follow the deer, even if you think you have missed.

A deer shot through the lungs usually goes off, after the first jump, as if nothing had happened to it. There is no variance in its trail from that of an uninjured deer, but alongside the trail there is in every case the story of where the bullet hit, in the shape of foamy, light-colored blood. This trail, too, may be followed immediately.

A liver shot is, perhaps, the least satisfactory of any. Sometimes the deer on being shot

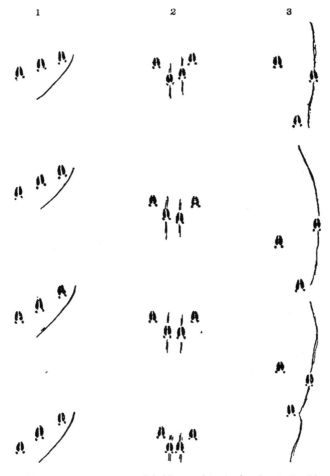

(1) Trail of a deer shot through brisket, and leg broken low in shoulder. (2) Trail of a deer shot through the shoulders high. (3) Trail of a deer with broken foreleg—the lower the leg is broken the more drag there is.

The shoulder shot (No. 2) should be followed immediately. It is best to shoot again when a deer gets up after the first shot strikes it here. They always drop like dead when shot thus.

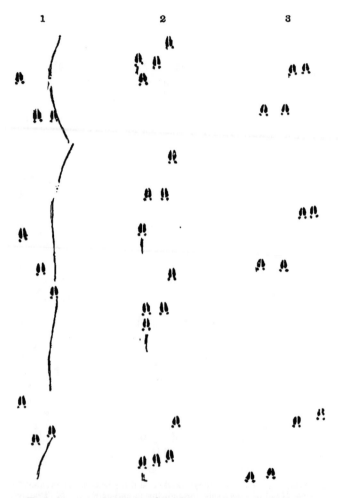

(1) Trail of a deer with broken hind leg—the lower the leg is broken the more drag there is. (2) Trail of a deer shot through the ham. (3) This trail usually means shot through intestines, liver and often lungs at the same time; the animal will not go much over a mile, even if not given time to get sick, and death results in less than two hours.

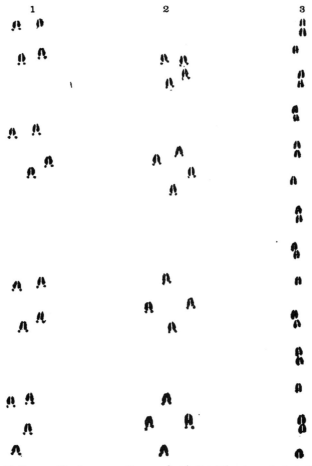

(1) Same as No. 3 on opposite page, but bullet did not penetrate to the
lungs. The animal dies slowly, and after a couple of hours is
usually shot in its bed. (2) The cross jump; result of a bullet
through intestines or liver when the animal was broadside to the
hunter—usually the slowest killing shot. (3) The tracks of a
wounded deer never register where the animal was walking.

All these curious jumps may be seen on one trail, alternating with jumps as made by
a sound deer. They indicate soft shots, and should not be followed within two hours
after the animal was shot. Blood, etc., on the trail decides for the tracker where the
bullet struck. Usually the less blood the surer the animal will be found dead after a
few hours.

through the liver, kicks, and at other times it humps itself up, but always it leaves the place at a quite lively rate, making a trail like a lung-shot deer, with here and there a cross jump between. (See illustration.) It is hard to advise what one should do in this case. I generally smoke a pipeful of tobacco before taking up the trail, to give the animal time to lie down. After that I follow and try to get another shot. While I have killed deer instantly with shots through the liver, there have been some that I never brought to bag.

Once I killed an elk three days after we had fried parts of its liver which had dropped out through the hole made by a projectile from a heavy-caliber English rifle, used previously for hunting elephants. At another time I killed a deer one year after having shot it through the liver. When killed, this deer was apparently as well and fat as could be, though in place of the soft liver we found a hard mass.

A shot through the intestines causes the animal to kick violently, hump up its back, and go off at a slow rate. It usually lies down within a quarter of a mile, and stays down if not molested too soon. Along the trail may be found a little dark-colored blood, and sometimes matter the animal has eaten. Deer shot thus should not be followed before at least two hours have passed, since if jumped they often go for miles. A deer with a broken leg may be followed at once, though the chase is usually quicker ended if half an hour is given for the animal to settle down.

In my opinion a sportsman who does any considerable hunting for big game should have his dog trained to follow a track as far as his master will follow him. A dog that runs deer is useless, and if he will not stay close to his master he must be kept on a leash. There is no law in any State against such use of a dog, and it would save much hard work to the man whose eye is not trained for tracking when there is no snow.

Besides the signs visible when a deer is shot, there are those which are brought to the hunter's knowledge through his ear: a hard, sharp sound conveying the intelligence that a bone is struck (and if it is not a leg the deer will hardly run), and a dull " thud " telling that a soft part is hit.

27

In any and every case the hunter should examine minutely the place where the game stood when it was shot at. The hair cut off by the bullet is often of great assistance in determining the location of the wound, and the torn-up needles or ground often show if the animal jumped or kicked as it was shot. Remember that the successful hunter is never in a hurry, and minutes spent in close observation will often save hours of exhausting chase.

Later in the season, when rough winds have robbed deciduous bushes of their leaves, bucks generally change their day stand, abandoning quaking-aspen thickets, and settling down among windfalls and small coniferous trees, thereby offering better chances for shots at any hour of the day. Still later, during the rutting season, the biggest specimens and best fighters will occupy those roomy, open forests, where in September and early October they make their appearance only during morning and evening hours. These old over-lords at this time select the places of a wider view, apparently to see others of their kind that may pass, to fight them

HOOF OF BLACK–TAILED DEER. (SLIGHTLY REDUCED)

off their range if they are bucks, and to claim ownership of them if they are does. The white-tail buck does not keep a harem, as is done by the elk and to some extent by the black-tailed deer, but stays with a doe a few days only, generally two or three, and then looks out for adventures elsewhere, or, more probably, the doe does not care for his company after being satisfied, and avoids him. Before the close of the hunting season, where it is extended until January 1, bucks again stay in thickets as prior to the rutting season, and soon after migrate to their winter range, where they, in company with does and fawns, spend the rigorous season of the year.

Summing up, we have seven signs by which to distinguish a buck's trail from that of a doe, of which the first in the following list is a feature of the white-tailed deer solely, and of which the three last named cannot be regarded as always absolutely certain:

1. Watching from cover;
2. Drag;
3. Blazing of trees;

4. Pawing of ground;
5. Distance of tracks from center line;
6. The pointing outward of toes;
7. The lagging back with the hind legs.

THE FAN-TAILED DEER

THE existence of the fan-tailed deer, or gazelle-deer, as it is sometimes called, is denied by some who know no better, but it is generally recognized by "old timers" and men who hunt it in its present restricted habitat. That its range was formerly more extensive than now, and that even now it still exists in widely separated districts, the writer infers from a letter of Justice Douglas, late of the Supreme Court of New York, whose guide apparently shot one in Michigan, and from an article in a sportsman's periodical by Mr. Ernest McGaffey, who found it in the Black Hills. The writer found relics of them in the Bad Lands of Montana and live specimens in the Snowy Mountains of the same State. It is evidently a smaller variety of the common Virginia deer, with a markedly longer tail; however, as its track shows some decided differences, by which it can readily

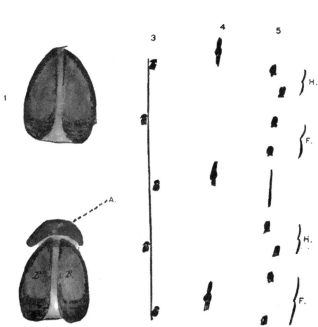

FAN–TAILED BUCK DEER. (ONE–HALF NATURAL SIZE)
(1) Front track. (2) Hind track. (3) Walk. (4) Trot. (5) Gallop.
(A) Dust heap. (B) Hillock.

be distinguished, it is considered advisable to treat it separately.

To begin with, the heels of the hoof are as broad as those of the Virginia deer, yet the hoof is considerably shorter, and consequently the track also, a feature which is, however, of value only on good tracking ground.

33.

The buck of this deer, whose tracks always register, walks with hoofs pressed close together, puts the heels firmly on the ground, which action moves the ground or snow toward the front, and steps off by making a deep imprint with the toes. The result is a small hillock in the middle of the track and, as this deer never drags its feet, a small dust heap in front of it. In snow or mud, of course, the latter sign cannot be found.

As this deer is much smaller than the ordinary white-tail, its steps are consequently shorter, and in loose snow, where no individual track is visible, its trail may be mistaken for that of a fawn, and only by following it a distance can an error be avoided.

Once a friend and I on our way home struck a trail, and while walking alongside it we both expressed our opinion that the deer which made it was the smallest fawn in that territory. We never would have given that trail any consideration had it not run along our path. As it was, we followed it, and after we had gone a hundred yards or so, my indifference changed to intense interest; for it could be seen that the deer had taken observations from nearly every shielding object it had passed. This caused me to express the belief that this deer was a very old fan-tailed buck, and events proved I was not mistaken. He had lost all his front teeth but two, which were badly used up, had four points on each antler, and weighed less than fifty pounds after his entrails were removed. As his conduct the day he was hunted down disclosed some features often experienced in the pursuit of deer, it is not out of place to relate it.

He was located in a thicket, and jumped with the assistance of the wind, a method which will be referred to later. We saw him but did not fire, as our chance opportunity was lost while we were looking for the horns so as to be sure not to kill a doe. His trail led to a creek two miles distant, and there disappeared. I knew that he had gone along in the creek, for wounded deer had often tricked me in that manner, but that a well deer should resort to that method to throw me off the track, after being so slightly molested, was rather astonishing. A quarter of a mile upstream I found where he had left the water, and

I followed the trail, having resolved that I would kill that buck in one way or another. The trail led me two miles farther, and then it stopped. The snow was like sand, and prevented the individual tracks from being seen plainly. The buck had back-tracked, and I had overrun the spot from which he made the side-jump. Back I went, and after going three hundred yards I found his artful side-jump, and the trail led into a thick clump of pines. Again I sent the wind in as a driver, and that time got a shot; but I did not down my quarry. The trail showed the buck was shot through the brisket and shoulder (low). Then I sat down, ate my lunch, and smoked my pipe. After that the trail led me again to the creek. I crossed to the other side and, about fifty yards from the creek, followed its course over half a mile, knowing that the buck would not leave the water on the side he entered it to lie down. Finally the creek led past a fir tree with low-hanging branches, and as the trail had not been seen thus far, I was moderately sure that the buck had not passed that cover—and it proved that he had not. During snowless times if a deer

DEER TRACKS

(1) Canter. (2) Going at a lively rate, in bounds up to twenty-four feet; lung-shot deer often run this way. (3) Top speed, bounds up to twenty-eight feet—indicates heart-shot if the animal is wounded.

has been wounded and gets away, hunting a day or two after along streams in the district will often bring to bay the wounded animal. If it has the strength, it will hunt up water to cool the wound, and then crawl into the densest cover that is near. I have found many deer in this way, dead and alive—and still more skeletons to which the tracks of "varmints" led me in the later season.

The signs of the fan-tailed buck are:

1. Watching from cover;
2. Hillock in track;
3. Dust heap in front of track;
4. Blazing of trees;
5. Pawing of ground.

38

THE MULE-DEER

THE track of the black-tailed or mule-deer, while it shows no appreciable differences from that of the Virginia (in white-tail country), undergoes—even in the mountains and breaks, its proper habitat—changes interesting not only to the student but to the hunter.

The three pictures of the hind foot of the same four-year-old mule-deer buck show what intermediate variations occur in the track of this animal. The photograph was taken when the buck was killed, and the drawings made in the rainy month of June, and at the time of the deer's death in October, respectively. That particular buck had its preferred stand on a lofty ridge, too high an altitude for white-tailed deer to make their permanent abode, though they frequent it as transient visitors.

The mule-deer always puts its foot down firmly from above, while the motion of the Virginia deer might be called rather one of sliding;

and because of this the hoofs spread sideways without lengthening the tracks. This gives the track of the latter a somewhat round appearance as long as there is moisture in the ground, or if it is covered by snow that is not too dry. This form of the track is usually found during the winter and early summer. Of course, when the rim becomes prominent enough to prevent spreading, as is the case during prolonged dry weather or in the arid regions, a big mule-deer will make a rather small track, and in many instances the sole of the hoof does not show at all in the mark. The track has very much the appearance of that made by a domestic sheep, yet it is different from it because in the sheep's track the heels and soles always show, and the hoofs are spread to an extent not found in deer. Besides, the halves of the hoof of a mule-deer are as a rule almost exactly alike, whereas with the sheep that is but seldom the case.

The buck of the mule-deer evidently has not sense enough to spend, for safety's sake, some of his time in watching from cover, and because of this his trail leads along without stopping, except

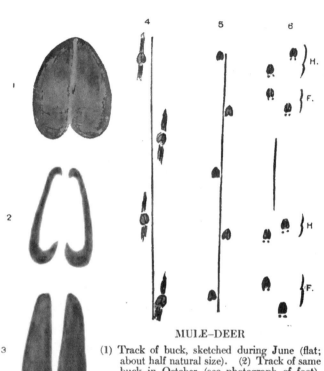

MULE–DEER

(1) Track of buck, sketched during June (flat; about half natural size). (2) Track of same buck in October (see photograph of foot). (3) Domestic sheep (flat). (4) Trail of buck; drag during rutting season from one step to the next. (5) Trail of doe. (6) Gallop.

where he did so to feed. Moreover, he does not vent his anger at a rival by pawing the ground as the white-tail buck does. As the rutting season of mule-deer is later in the year, the drag in the buck's trail is a most prominent feature, when in the case of the Virginia deer it has ceased to connect the individual tracks.

In determining whether one stands before the trail of a mule-deer or some other kind, the locality where the track is found has to be considered, which often solves the question. Their natural habitat is usually higher mountains, and even the treeless breaks where no white-tailed deer are to be found. The possibility of confounding a big mule-deer track with a small elk track is not remote; however, if one observes closely, mistakes will not occur often, as the young elk places his feet nearer the center line under the body than an old mule-deer buck, and never makes any drag. Then again a full-grown elk always makes a track at least twice the size of that of the mule-deer.

The signs of the mule-deer buck are:

1. Drag;
2. Blazing of trees;
3. Distance of tracks from center line;
4. Pointing outward of toes.

42

THE WAPITI OR ELK

IN the pursuit of *Cervus canadensis* the aim of the tracker is to distinguish the signs of the bull from those of the cow. As the number to be killed per season by each hunter is limited by law to one or two bulls, the pursuer is naturally interested in knowing how to tell the signs of the old ones.

They are:

1. Size of track;
2. Distance of track from center line;
3. Pointing outward of hoofs;
4. Hillock in track;
5. Lagging back with hind legs;
6. Closeness of track;
7. Roundness of toes;
8. Blazing of trees;
9. Pawing of ground;
10. Size and roundness of dew-claws.

43

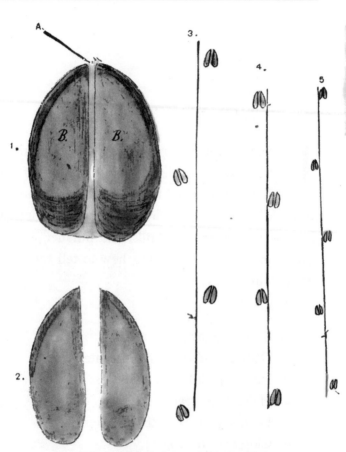

ELK. (ONE–HALF NATURAL SIZE)
(1) Bull track. (A) Closeness of track. (B) Hillock. (2) Cow track, flat (note spread). (3) Trail of bull. (4) Trail of cow. (5) Trail of calf.

A male yearling has a bigger hoof, and consequently makes a larger track, than a female of

6

7

H {

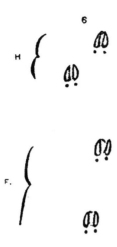

F.

H {

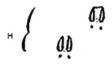

F {

ELK
(6) Gallop.   (7) Trot.

the same age, and as the track of a three-year-old bull is the size of that of a large cow, it is obvious that even the track of the largest sterile specimen of the hornless sex cannot approach in size that made by an old bull. As the general size of the elk differs in their various districts, this fact has to be considered; an elk in the Coast country, for example, is much inferior in weight to an elk of the same age in the Rockies. For this reason it is necessary to know the general size of the elks in the territory in which the tracking is done to estimate with approximate correctness the number of points on their horns from the size of the track.

The bigger the bull, the farther, of course, stand the tracks away from the center line. What has been said about this, and about the pointing outward of toes in the chapter on Virginia deer, applies also to the elk, with the difference, however, that in the latter it is always a *sure* sign of the bull, as is also the lagging back with the hind feet.

Like the fan-tail buck, the elk bull, in his manner of walking, makes a hill in his track, but there is no dust heap in front of the latter's, as the elk apparently does not step off so clean.

The bull elk always manages to walk with tightly closed hoofs, at variance with the cow, which lets the hoofs spread more.

By reason of his weight and his habit of pawing the ground, the points of the hoofs or toes of an old bull become rather blunt, causing a much rounder track than a cow makes; and in a big track, like that of an elk, such features show up conspicuously, while it would be a hard matter to detect them in a much smaller deer track, even on the best tracking ground.

The dew-claws, being much thicker and blunter in the bull than in the cow, are a certain distinctive feature, but their imprint. can be seen only in mud or snow, and there the other more prominent signs of the bull track are, as a rule, visible also and will be found more reliable.

The young bull often oversteps the forefoot track with the hind foot; therefore in case the tracks do not register it is necessary to examine the two individual tracks of one side. If the bigger track is in front, an old bull made it, and if the reverse is the case, the animal is not worth following, because it is a young one.

Like all members of the deer tribes, the elk bull cleanses his horns of the velvet on trees, and, in addition to pawing the ground with the hoofs, he often belabors it with his horns in his anger with a rival.

Some consider the distance between the individual tracks in the attempt to determine the size and other points of the elk, and if the animal has been seen, this is well, but if there is only the trail to decide by, it appears to be a far-fetched " sign," because the foundation, a knowledge of the speed, is lacking.

THE MOOSE

THE favorite rendezvous, in summer or winter range, of any other member of the deer tribes may be ascertained by the observant trailer, and the animal found within a given area with moderate certainty, but not so our most gigantic game, the moose; he is far too much of a traveler. True, he too has his range, but its limits are so extended that he may return to the same place but once within a month or two. Here to-day and elsewhere to-morrow seems to be his rule.

Yet, in spite of the moose's habits, the tracker may bag him in any given locality by ascertaining in what umbrageous thicket or on what wooded hillside the moose prefers to stay during his visits, that is, if the hunter does not wish to run him down by sheer endurance, which would take him over deep, crusted snow, cost about a week's hard work, and furnish poor sport.

On account of its extraordinary size, it is out
of the question that the track of a bull moose
should be mistaken for that of another deer;
rather it might be taken for that of a big ox,
except the track of the latter is always rounder
and the entire hoof-form different.   Where any
doubt exists, a close examination will invariably
dispel it.   In forming a conclusion about a moose
track the chief aim is always to decide if it was
made by a bull or cow.   The hoof of the bull is
bulkier than that of the cow, and should therefore
produce a rounder track.   The immense weight
of the animal tends to obliterate such minor distinctive features in most cases where the ground
is not very hard.

The dew-claws on the bull are always farther
apart than on the cow, and as they are much
blunter they make a good mark to consider.

The individual tracks of the bull are farther
off from the center line than in the case of the
cow; but as the stride is long, this feature is not
apparent to any appreciable extent.

The length of the steps, if it is possible to
estimate the gait he was traveling from his other

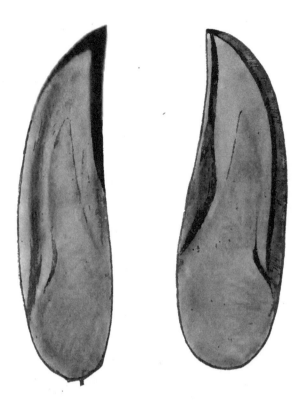

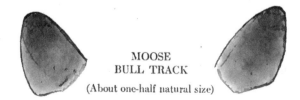

**MOOSE
BULL TRACK**

(About one-half natural size)

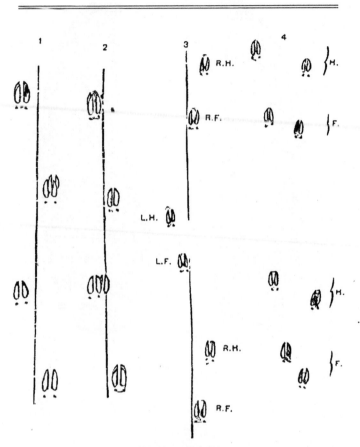

MOOSE TRACKS
(1) Trail of bull.   (2) Trail of cow.   (3) Trot.   (4) Gallop.

actions (feeding, etc.), is one of the best signs of the bull, since he makes markedly longer strides than the cow of equal size.

From all the foregoing it is obvious that it is a rather doubtful possibility for the beginner to tell the track of a bull from that of a cow, but actual observations in the woods will impart to him the ability to distinguish between them with a considerable degree of accuracy. Until he so learns he should follow every likely looking track until it enters a thicket, and if he is following a bull with a halfway good set of horns he will notice overhead broken twigs and bent branches, or perhaps he will find along the trail blazed trees, broken bushes, or the ground torn with hoofs or horns, and may know by these also that a bull made the signs.

Unlike any other deer previously discussed, the moose, when trotting, oversteps the forefeet tracks with the hind feet to a considerable extent. (See sketch of trail.)

As signs of the bull moose we may consider:

1. Roundness of hoof;
2. Distance between and bluntness of dewclaws;
3. Distance of tracks from center line;

4. Length of steps;

5. Breaking of twigs with horns (overhead along trail) ;

6. Blazing of trees;

7. Pawing of ground.

THE MOUNTAIN SHEEP

Where first the early sunbeams glow
On rugged cliffs, through morning shrouds,
Where icy winds in summer blow
On crests among the thunder clouds,
Way up on mountains high and steep,
There lives and roams the bighorn sheep.

THE king of sports, undoubtedly, is the pursuit of the bighorn, but on account of the habitat of this game, under normal conditions, it is restricted to comparatively few hunters, since perfect physical condition and unswerving perseverance are required to endure the hardships which present themselves in mountain climbing and " camping out of camp," and to bear cheerfully the many discouraging experiences which are commonly the lot of the sportsman who desires to secure the finest trophy to be taken in our country.

No other reminder of the chase will bring back to memory so many pleasant recollections as the head and horns of an old mountain ram after time has obliterated the memory of the hardships endured, and has woven around the trophy a halo through which the mind's eye sees again sublime views from lofty mountain peaks, roseate dawns and glowing sunsets, which bathed cliffs and crests and crags in a flood of molten gold. Again the hunter feels the thrill of care-free independence of the trifling world below, and experiences boundless elation as the crack of the rifle, sounding and resounding from a thousand crags, proclaims to the Alpine world the triumphant end of the chase.

The tracking of this game consists chiefly in locating it by the signs left on high meadows, or near springs or salt-licks. Except for the larger spoor of the ram, there is no difference in the track or trail of either sex.

Generally on meadows or near springs, where the big tracks of a single animal, or at most a couple of them, are frequently found, and where the tracks of lambs are conspicuous by their absence, one may expect, with moderate certainty, to see game worthy of a shot, as rams prefer to

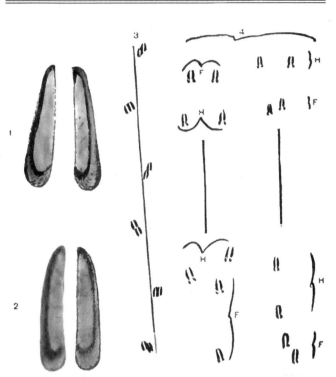

MOUNTAIN SHEEP. (ONE–HALF NATURAL SIZE)
(1) Front track. (2) Hind track. (3) Trail. (4) Leaps.

range alone, except at rutting time and during the winter.

If there is no snow, one may learn to know the track of every individual sheep which frequents the range, and if he spends much time there he will see an animal at too great a distance to be

57

shot at, but if he has any memory at all, he will recognize its track if he finds it anywhere in that region. This, of course, does not refer to mountain sheep below the average, which, I assume, are of little interest to the sportsman who takes the trouble to hunt for a trophy; nor does the meat hunter go up into these regions for the pot, as he will get something easier lower down.

If the feeding ground or watering place of an old ram is once known, about the best thing to do is to wait for the quarry. If the game is seen, and it has not already observed the hunter, it usually can be flagged as antelopes were in former days. The oldest bucks, however, seldom respond to the 'summons, and are seldom lured within rifle range by this method.

Hunting bighorn has much in common with hunting antelopes, but in the pursuit of the former there is grander scenery and more physical exercise.

The tracks of mountain sheep often show the cross-step, seldom register, and, as the animals when running have to place their feet where they can, the trail gives no indication of where an ani-

HOG TRACK; WALKING. (ABOUT HALF NATURAL SIZE)

To save the novice from ridiculous experiences this illustration is given. The hog track is always spread, very seldom registers, and, if the ground is not very hard, the dew-claws are always shown.

mal has been hit. Infinitely greater vigilance is required than in deer hunting to observe the signs at the moment of firing, and in the study of hair and blood.

The hoof of the bighorn spreads easily and evenly; therefore, in the track the distance between the heels is as great as between the toes, and frequently greater—a fact which makes it impossible to confound it with that of any other animal.

As stated, there is but one sign by which to tell the ram: Size of·the track.

THE ANTELOPE

THE track of the antelope looks like a combination of a bighorn track, which it resembles somewhat in length and prominence of the outer rim of the hoof, and that of the domestic sheep, to which it bears a likeness in the shape of the heels. To confound it, however, with either one of them is a rather remote possibility, since the heels are broader and closer together than those of a mountain sheep, with which in the Bad Lands the antelope is sometimes found in the same range, and the spread is different from that of the domestic sheep. In the case of the domestic sheep the greatest spread is at the point of the toes, while in the case of the antelope, the hoof being hooked, it is more between the soles.

An antelope buck of moderate size makes at all times a bigger track than any range sheep, the track of the latter always being rather flat. As antelopes live on the open plains where they are generally hunted by sighting them, and as a sportsman is allowed to kill but one in a season, we will therefore consider only the signs of the old bucks.

There are but two signs, and these can be condensed into one, because they are usually found at the same spot: Pawing of ground, and droppings.

The droppings are of similar size, and though more or less connected, always comparatively dry, while from does and fawns they are either dry and scattered, or, if moist, in a lump and always irregular in size; the cause of which seeming phenomenon is a certain amount of glutinous substance in the droppings of the buck.

The pawing is usually done in old buffalo trails, cattle runways, and roads, or where coal deposits come to the surface making the ground barren of vegetation; where this sign is found, an old buck is always near, even if the locality cannot properly be considered antelope country. Old bucks, before and after rutting season, frequently make their habitat in roomy forests or

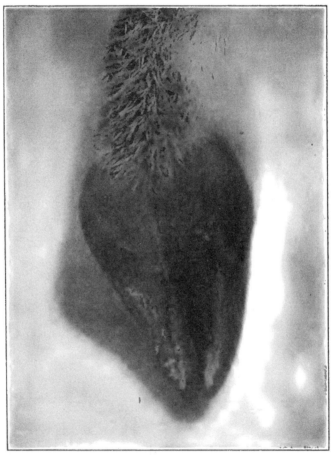

HIND FOOT OF ANTELOPE. (LIFE SIZE)

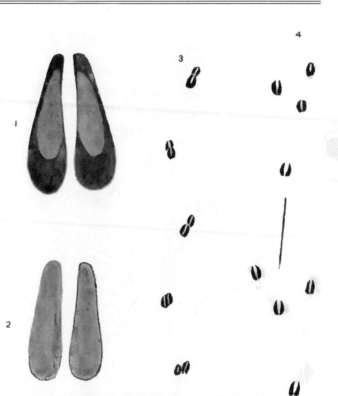

ANTELOPE.   (ONE–HALF NATURAL SIZE)

(1) Track of antelope.   (2) Domestic sheep (flat), note spread.   (3) Trail of antelope.   (4) Gallop (no dew-claws; the antelope has none).

in the breaks of the Bad Lands, sometimes several miles distant from the grounds where the herds roam.

The rutting season begins about the middle of

THE SIGN OF THE ANTELOPE (BUCK)

August. The old bucks are first in selecting their does, but they have to leave their respective adherents on account of the stronger young bucks, which fight off their old and emaciated rivals. During the rutting season all bucks have such an emphatically disagreeable odor that it is absolutely impossible to eat the meat; afterward they are but skin and bones, and before they can pick up again and are fit for food, they shed their horns. The sportsman, in consequence of the law, which opens the shooting season for antelope September 1st, is put to two disagreeable alternatives: either to shoot a buck and let the meat rot, saving horns and skin as a trophy of the sport (?), or to kill a doe or fawn, to feast on excellent venison, and incidentally hasten the extermination of the most beautiful creature of the plains.

Sport with antelope bucks in the full sense of the word, can be had only during the summer months; then they tax the hunter's skill, and their meat is fit for the table of an epicure.

When their natural range is absorbed by private preserves, or when human progress is advanced so far that it demands even of politicians the exercise of some common sense, then, no doubt, laws will be passed befitting the game. Until then, the sportsman, to keep his shield of honor bright, must abstain from the killing of antelope; else, ridiculous and inconsistent as it may seem, if he decides he must have a trophy of this kind, in any event, he must disregard the statutory laws.

Flagging old bucks seems to me an inexcusable waste of time; those which I have tried to flag have invariably heeded the signal, and left immediately for distant ranges, apparently having profited from previous experiences.

The distress cry of a jack-rabbit, however, invariably causes antelope to investigate. Often when I have been calling for wolves and coyotes, antelopes have appeared seemingly from nowhere and approached so close that they could easily have been killed with a shotgun. If there is a herd of cattle in the known range of an old buck it is almost a sure thing that he will associate with them during the late afternoon. In timbered country bucks will be found frequenting comparatively small parks where it is easy to stalk them.

The antelope has the widest range of vision of all our game, but like the others it is unable to distinguish objects when looking toward the sun, a fact which at times has its advantages when hunting the antelope or bighorn sheep.

The wound-signs are the same as in deer; but as antelope are usually shot at in open country, they can generally be seen until they drop dead or lie down. In the latter case it is more merciful to let them die without disturbing them, unless it is possible from the lay of the country to stalk them so that their misery may be ended by a second well-aimed shot.

By reason of the hoof-form, the very prominent hillock in the antelope track is of no value in ascertaining the sex, and neither is the irregular stepping in the trail.

Animal	Size of Track	Distance from Center Line	Pointing Outward of Hoofs	Hillock in Track	Drag	Lagging Back of Hind Legs	Clearness of Track	Round-ness of Toes	Size and Form of Dew Claws	Blazing of Trees	Pawing of Ground
Virginia Deer	−	+	+	−	+	+	*Watching from cover*	*Watching from cover*		+	+
Fan-Tailed Deer	*Dust heap in front of track*	+	+	+	−	−	*Watching from cover*			+	+
Mule Deer	−	+	+	−	+	−	−	−	−	+	−
Elk	+	+	+	+	−	+	+	+	+	+	+
Moose	−	+	*Length of steps* / *Breaking of twigs with horns*		−	−	−	+	+	+	+
Big-Horn	+	−	−	−	−	−	−	−	−	−	−
Antelope	+	−	−	−	*Droppings*		−	−	−	−	+

PREDACEOUS ANIMALS

THE BEAR

HUNTING bears with the assistance of guides supplied with a well-trained pack of hounds may be satisfactory, if merely the killing of them is desired, but it certainly is not sport, and does not even deserve to be ranked with trapping bears, as in the latter case the hunter must possess at least some knowledge of the quarry's habitat and habits. Unlike a fox, , a bear when once found by the hounds stands no chance of escaping, and there would be just as much sport in shooting the animal in a park or pen as in killing a run-to-bay bear. This applies also with truth to mountain lions, although perhaps there is in the case of the cougar the excuse of the animal's destructiveness.

The employment of dogs in the chase would never exterminate or even appreciably lessen the number of deer in any hunting country where lakes are not abundant, but everywhere it surely means the downfall and extinction of that relic of gray ages, the bear.

Where not plentiful—and the places where they are found in number are to-day quite few and remote from civilization—bears are, on the whole, harmless, and decidedly more useful than injurious. The damage they do is almost *nil,* while they serve man in many ways. The meat of young bears is equal to the best venison; their fat is decidedly superior to the " fancy " lard we buy, of the source and handling of which we are ignorant; and the hides give excellent service as robes, rugs and clothing. In my opinion bears should be protected to a certain extent rather than shot down merely to make a record.

Sport should be conducted in a spirit of fairness to the game, and while a couple of dogs is perhaps permissible in bear hunting, still-hunting is the better sport, because it requires the utmost skill and knowledge of woodcraft on account of the quarry's sagacity and cunning, which is superior to that of any other of our wild animals. Even if one is able to read the habits of the bear clearly from its trail, it is necessary to pos-

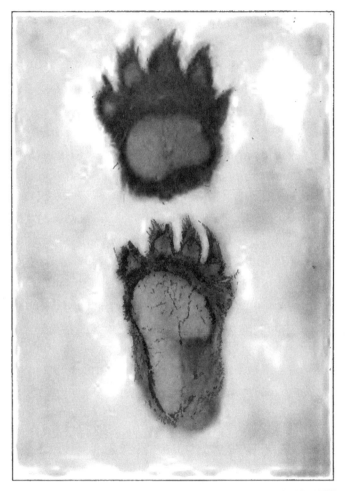

BEAR FEET—RIGHT SIDE (ONE-QUARTER NATURAL SIZE)

sess an abundant supply of patience, for, barring lucky accidents, no one can reasonably hope to outwit Bruin at the first attempt.

The end of their hibernation depends largely on the weather, but about March or April bears frequent snowless slopes and gulches in search of roots, bulbs, and similar food, and it is there one must look for signs at that time. If a cold spell interrupts the spring weather, as is often the case, a trail, sometimes a week old, will often lead the hunter to a near-by thicket where Bruin has made himself a bed on the ground, with the intention of sleeping until another thaw. He usually changes his bed every two or three days, but ordinarily will not leave the thicket unless he is disturbed. If a bear is found to be in such a thicket, the hunter should curb his impatience and suspend following up the trail until the snow gets soft, when he can work carefully against the wind toward his quarry. However, as it is usually impossible to see farther than ten or twenty feet ahead, Bruin has, in this kind of hunting, much the best of the hunter, and the latter finds in most cases an empty bed.

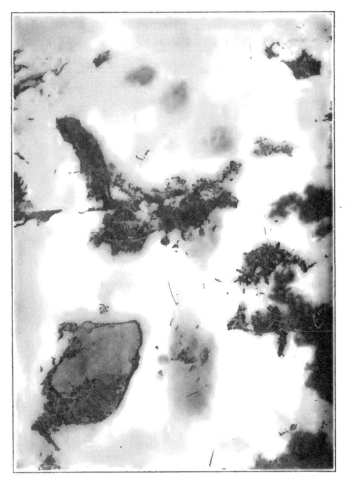

BEAR TRAIL. (STEPS ABOUT TWO FEET APART)

If the thicket is not too large the wind-hunting method before described will, no doubt, often give satisfaction; but as a rule the thickets which the bears make their spring habitat are of too great an extent. The surest and easiest way to get him is to persuade some other fellow to follow the trail while you intercept and shoot the bear when he leaves the thicket. Knowledge of Bruin's cunning then furnishes the means to decide where he will pass, since, as a rule, he will sneak off under the densest cover and try to reach another thicket under shelter of bushes, rocks and the like. Anyone, not altogether a tyro in the woods, can easily decide from the lay of the country where to wait for His Bearship. When the place is selected, one should be sure that there is an absolutely clear opening at least a couple of feet wide. A bear is bulky and clumsy-looking enough, but he is able to pass without offering a chance for a shot at places where another animal could hardly escape an average hunter's lead. I am by no means slow with my trigger finger, but before I learned to appreciate this fact I was chagrined on several occasions by hav-

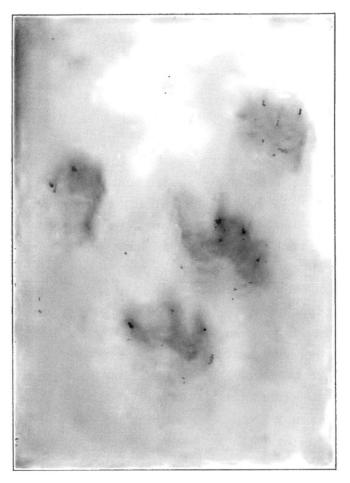

TRACKS OF BEAR, RUNNING

ing bears pass me unharmed at a less distance than fifty yards, and that too at places where I thought I could kill a running rabbit if I wished to do so.

If a bear succeeds in leaving a thicket without giving opportunity for a shot, there is no need for disappointment—he will pass the same spot when he happens to be in the same thicket again, and this is a certainty if he does not abandon that part of the country. This statement has met with some disbelief among a few of my personal acquaintances, and to prove my claims I had to shoot a bear within a month from a given point. I killed Bruin, or rather Old Eph, as it was a grizzly, less than ten feet from where I said I would, and that settled the matter.

A mile and a half from my home there is such a thicket not over one acre in extent, and if fresh bear signs are seen anywhere in the surrounding woods, which cover several thousand acres and contain many larger and just as dense thickets, I wait there, reasonably sure that I will see Bruin soon after sunrise or at sunset. Experience has proved to me that it is a waste of time to watch

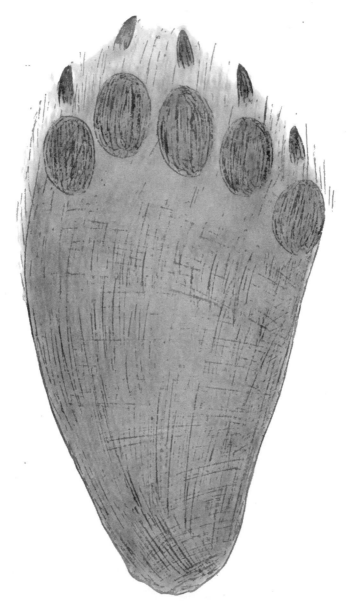

BEAR TRACK. (HIND FOOT; TWO-THIRDS NATURAL SIZE)

for bears where signs are most numerous. They invariably leave their home thicket very quietly before dark, and start their noisy feeding, chewing up logs, and breaking down berry bushes, not less than half a mile from their abiding place, near which no signs except a few tracks are visible.

For the entertainment of a visiting friend the thicket was driven a few times by the wind method, which worked splendidly. An "old mule," which was shot through the lungs with a .30-40 rifle on the previous evening, was the only one that left the shelter slowly. All the others, presumably the same on every occasion, appeared to be very much frightened, and ran for about three-quarters of a mile after they had passed the danger point

To locate the abode of bears in such thickets during the summer and early autumn, it is best and simplest to trail them by the signs they make during their nocturnal rambles, such as overturned logs, etc.; and if only a few of such signs are found near dense cover, facing north or northwest, the ground should be carefully ex-

BEAR STUMP. (ANTS WERE CHEWED OUT SEVEN
FEET ABOVE GROUND)

amined for tracks. These are usually difficult
to see, and if no moist places are near such cover,
the apparently used paths that lead into it, but
on which there are no signs except an occasional

83

claw mark, must serve as base for a conclusion, which must be verified by watching at a good point near the thicket during the morning or evening. The snapping of a twig or the break- ing of a log on which Bruin carelessly steps often confirms the conclusions, though the bear may sometimes remain invisible to the hunter for sev- eral consecutive visits.

When the thicket they prefer is once located, the rest is easy. If quick results are desired, driving or, perhaps, calling will yield results. I once shot a bear which made its appearance im- mediately when, by way of experiment, I imi- tated the distress cry of a jack-rabbit. If the hunter has plenty of time to spend in the woods it is a good plan to watch for the quarry. Dur- ing autumn proper, bears retreat to the more remote districts and the fastnesses of the moun- tains; here they are usually found during the day- time where they are accustomed to feed. In places where berries are plentiful, on ridges and in gulches where blue jays and squirrels are stor- ing their winter supply of mast, here will be found the bears' favorite autumn haunts. In

BEAR TRACK. (FRONT FOOT; ABOUT TWO–FIFTHS
NATURAL SIZE)

the mountains of the West there is a berry bush
called kinni-kinic barberry or bearberry—I am
not sure which is the correct term—that is thickly
covered with fruit about the size of buffalo berries, and which is a favorite food for bears before
they can obtain mast; or, if the latter fails, Bruin
seems to regard the seeds of the piñon as a deli-
cacy; but as it would apparently take up too
much of his time to fill himself from those that
fall to the ground, he resorts to easier methods
to obtain them—he becomes a thief and incurs
the enmity of squirrels and jays.

On ridges he robs the caches of the jays, and
in cañons he depletes the stores of the squirrels,
and, by no means approving of such actions, they
heartily hate him and " cuss " at him whenever
he approaches, and in this way often betray his
presence to the hunter who has learned to interpret the language of the wood-folk. It is always
well to approach with the utmost care places
where there is a continual chatter of squirrels and
cries of blue jays are heard; and if the " cussed "
one proves to be some other marauder—well, it
may be a bear next time. When still-hunting

BEAR LOG

during the autumn the attention paid to these
small denizens of the woods is by no means wasted,
and yields better results than covering a great
territory, or watching for hours on trails or near
baits, which latter are seldom visited by bears
during rifle light.

Until I undertook the systematic study of the
bear's habits I was under the impression, from
what I had read, that a bear track was easily

87

recognized, and actually passed many, regarding them as cougar tracks. I have since noticed that many hunters, born and reared in a bear country, make the same mistake. Of course in mud or snow a bear track is easily identified, but in the vastness of mountains and forests snow and mud are not always present; in fact, they are of little service. There, the heel of the foot is practically never seen in the track during snowless times, and as the shape of the fore part of the foot conforms with that of the mountain lion, a mistake is easily possible if the imprints of the five toes of the bear are not all visible. The trailer in these districts and under these circumstances is generally lucky if he can discern here and there the part of a track of a bear's foot. A couple of years ago a party of old deer hunters told me of the great number of lion tracks they had seen as they came into camp, and at my query if they saw any bear tracks, they answered, " No "; yet I had camped there over two months, knew absolutely that no lion was in those parts, that bears were abundant, and that the hunters could have seen only their tracks. So

BEAR LOG

much for the information of those who have an idea that an animal, weighing from three hundred to over a thousand pounds, must necessarily make a big trail which can be readily followed.

The tracker, if he will but stop and investigate closely, need not make a mistake, even if only the imprint of a single toe is plainly visible, as the long nails of the bear almost always leave some mark in front of the track. The distance

89

which the nails stand away from the toe imprints is the only means of distinguishing the grizzly's track from that of the black bear, except that size dispels any doubt. The nails of the grizzly stand out almost straight, while those of the black bear are more curvate, and their imprints must consequently be found closer to the track of the foot.

The likeness of the bear track to that of the human foot has been referred to by many writers. In reality no likeness exists, and the inexperienced trailer in the woods has the already disadvantageous conditions under which he is working multiplied so long as he is not disillusioned.

If a bear who knows nothing of the hunter is shot at and suddenly whirls around, *i. e.*, jumps when the trigger is pulled, he is hit, no matter whether there is another sign or not, and the color of the blood will indicate to the hunter where he is struck. A shot through the lungs with the modern high-power rifle will sometimes not prove fatal within ten or twelve hours.

A missed bear is never in a hurry to get away, unless he has seen or scented the hunter previous to the firing, and in most cases he offers a chance for a second or third shot.

Not a few city hunters " pull out " if they en-counter bear signs where they intend to spend their outing, saying they are not looking for bears; yet the chances are many against their seeing one even if they were anxious for an en-counter. The trouble is not to avoid a bear, but to find him, as his greatest desire seems to be to keep out of man's reach, and he employs all his cunning to that end.

THE COUGAR

OF all the predatory animals there is none which in destructiveness equals or even approaches the mountain lion; he, and he only, is often the cause of unsatisfactory hunting trips into districts where other big game by every reason ought to be abundant. A family of these great beasts will, while the young ones are growing up, deplete a region of almost every other game animal.

If a cougar kills a deer during the morning hours, he seems to spend the day near it, as I have again and again found freshly vacated beds under nearby bushes or rocks. On these occasions I was following the drag the " varmint " had made with the carcass, and although I kept a close watch on the surroundings, the lion remained invisible; yet I know that he was watching me, for in every instance I found that he visited and examined the covered carcass during the following night. '

The methods usually followed to rid the hunting-ground of its worst poacher are to shoot or trap him. If the former is decided upon, the fact that the lion has an excellent nose and keen vision should not be forgotten when the place to watch for him is selected.

Still-hunting the cougar is about the most thankless undertaking one could enter upon, yet there are occasions when a close observer may be able to kill one without extra trouble when out primarily for other game. The main requisite is time and a thorough acquaintance with the country. The cougar, after the young are grown up, does not remain in a comparatively small district for any length of time, but usually covers a much wider territory than the gray wolf, although the latter is universally known as a great wanderer. At irregular intervals, say from once in a fortnight to once in two months, depending on the region, it returns to the same district. Unlike the wolf, the cougar, in returning to and hunting over a district, does not usually go over the same trail and buttes he has used on the previous trip, but prefers to explore new ground on each occa-

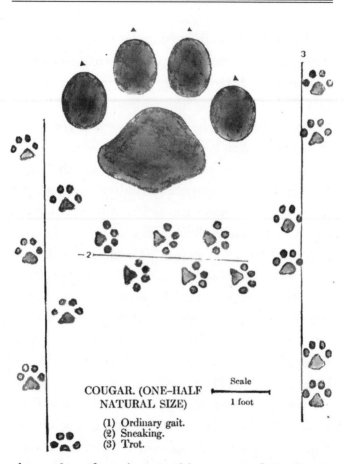

COUGAR. (ONE–HALF
NATURAL SIZE)

Scale

1 foot

(1) Ordinary gait.
(2) Sneaking.
(3) Trot.

sion unless there is something unusual to attract
him. If his tracks, therefore, are seen quite often
on a certain lookout point, the hunter should be
alert for the cause of attraction, generally a

fallen tree, or an overhanging rock protecting a snug dry bed beneath from rain or snow, which are always situated on a wind-sheltered hillside facing south. When such a place is known, the hunter should scrupulously refrain from going near it, to avoid leaving any scent there; but he should observe the " nest " as often as he comes into its vicinity, and from a convenient distant point. If the " nest " has an occupant, it is better to let a bullet investigate before the hunter does so himself, for a cat is a cat, and if its suspicions are aroused, the devil cannot beat it in trickiness—it will vanish unobserved without the hunter knowing how it could have done so. I once shot one out of a bunch of three, and felt sure the remaining two were " my meat," yet not a spot of yellow of them did I see afterward, although every nook within three hundred yards of the surrounding country was seemingly open to my scouting.

This is tedious hunting, of course, and the number of cougars would not be appreciably lessened by the method; but one lion outwitted thus is worth perhaps, as a trophy of skill, a score killed by other means; and besides, it at least gives the still-hunter a chance.

Cougars do not respond readily to being called (by imitating the cries of a jack-rabbit) ; at least I have lured but one in eight or ten years, and missed it at that. Trapping them is as sure as gambling, *i. e.*, there is never any certainty that one will get the lion, and as their existence is unquestionably obnoxious to sportsmen and stockgrowers alike, hunting them with dogs is a commendable method, since it insures their decrease, and to the tyro means a trophy.

Barnyard study is, undoubtedly, responsible for the conclusions advanced by some writers that the members of the cat family are the most perfect track makers, *i. e.*, walkers. As a matter of fact, the trail of a wild cat cannot be compared, so far as perfection goes, with the trail of the wild dog. The cougar's tracks seldom register. He either oversteps with the hind foot the track made by the forefoot when in a hurry, or he does not step quite far enough to cover the forefoot track when leisurely walking, and the individual tracks do not stand so close to the center

96

line of the trail as do those of the wolf. The roundness of the track, together with the inconspicuousness of the nail marks, even under the most favorable tracking conditions, makes the cougar track unmistakably different from that of a wolf. However, on hard ground the track of a bear and a lion may be easily taken for one another, though the latter contains but four toe-marks. But then every toe-mark is not often visible on hard ground.

With all predatory animals the rule holds good that the female track appears smaller than that of the male, even though the size of the animals be the reverse. For example, a male cougar measuring seven feet from tip to tip, will make a bigger track than a nine-foot-long female. Although with dividers and tape-line one might have difficulty to ascertain the difference, which at best would be very small to the eye, it is unmis-takable, and one well acquainted with tracks can hardly make the error of mistaking a female track for that of a male. The latter always looks more substantial.

It is the same with the tracks of males and

females of predatory animals as it is with a
bunch of deer, or of a single one for that matter, after bucks have shed their horns. The initiated can tell accurately from the appearance
of the animals which are bucks and which are
does; yet if questioned *how* he knows it, he
can scarcely answer. At best he will say, "Because it looks like one." The reason for my
dwelling on this subject is by no means an idle
one. During the early summer the ravages of
"varmints" often become almost unbearable to
stockmen, and since females, which have to pro-
vide for their offspring, are the worst offenders,
it is well for anyone to be able to distinguish their
tracks from those of males, in order to follow
them only, as they are the only ones that will
always with certainty lead to the den within a
day's travel.

Predatory animals are, in the writer's opinion,
not monogamous. While a male is often found
with a family, the same male may be seen the
next day with others of his kind miles away. I
have noted this while following game on horse-
back. On the other hand, a male track may lead

to several dens if followed far enough. On several occasions I have shot two or even three males of a species near a den within a week or so, the desire to kill the female being on every occasion responsible for the long-continued watch.

In following a track with the purpose of hunting up a den it makes but little difference whether the trail be fresh or old. A trail two weeks old, but made after a rain, is often more easily followed than a fresher one, and will as well lead to the den's vicinity, as the latter very often could not be followed at all on hard ground; and a back-trail often leads more quickly to the den than one leading ahead. Prevailing conditions of weather and lay of country should govern the tracker's choice of which trail to follow. He must know that he has to follow the back track if it comes from rough country, for the den is more likely situated there than elsewhere.

A den that contains young cougars is readily recognized by the superabundance of carcasses of game lying around its vicinity.

Certainly unless due regard is given to the extermination of predatory animals, it is impos-

99

sible to bring a hunting preserve up to the highest standard, and for the same reason their unrestricted existence in the open hunting grounds can only be harmful. The time when predatory animals kept the number of other game in a healthy balance has passed, and the sportsman who kills half a dozen deer ought to have to his credit at least one member of the former tribe to offset his killing those of the latter. As few of the hunting fraternity attain this desirable result, I think those who kill as many or more marauders as they do useful game animals, ought to be hailed as benefactors to the sportsmen's fraternity. Sometimes, I am sorry to say, such an action is referred to as unsportsmanlike by those who would soon find the woods empty of desirable game if others gave no more attention to marauders than they do themselves.

THE LYNX

WHAT the cougar is as an enemy to the useful big game, the bob-cat is to small game and the young of big game. He, however, lacks the cunning of the former, being easily called or trapped, and therefore as a class, and excepting individual cases few and far between, will never become a menace to either the sportsmen's fraternity or to stockgrowers. Where hundreds of them infest the country—as in certain sections of the Bad Lands—they only serve to check the increase of the millions of cottontail rabbits, which would otherwise so rapidly multiply that they would become a destructive pest throughout the cultivated sections of the country.

The tracker, trailing bob-cats like deer, can often surprise them at prowling, or jump them at close range from their beds, which are usually found under deadfalls or overhanging rocks, etc. Until their suspicions are aroused they are very

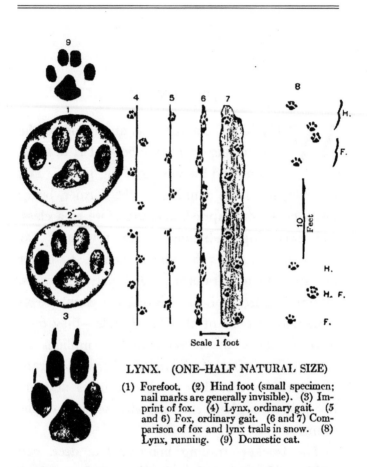

Scale 1 foot

LYNX. (ONE–HALF NATURAL SIZE)

(1) Forefoot. (2) Hind foot (small specimen;
nail marks are generally invisible). (3) Imprint of fox. (4) Lynx, ordinary gait. (5
and 6) Fox, ordinary gait. (6 and 7) Comparison of fox and lynx trails in snow. (8)
Lynx, running. (9) Domestic cat.

foolish and the writer has shot not a few with a
.22 rifle when still-hunting for rabbits. When
called, they have not sense enough to run away
if missed by the first and even second shot. In

RIGHT FRONT PAW OF LYNX

hunting them with dogs they give good sport, and
not infrequently get away by entering holes or
putting the dogs to shame in some other manner.

103

RED LYNX

At a careless glance the lynx track is but a miniature of that of the cougar, but a close examination reveals the fact that the marks of the individual toes are proportionately much more elongated than in the latter. The trail, though

104

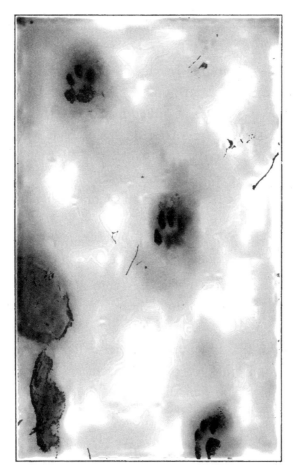

LYNX TRAIL

much better than the mountain lion's trail, is not as perfect as that of the coyote or fox, for either of which it might be mistaken in loose snow; it is always more out of line. In *Country Life in America* for June, 1905, a well-known nature writer shows a lynx trail, as perfectly as it can be illustrated, as that of a fox. With such good standing tracks it is inexcusable if the trailer makes a mistake, and even if one has had but little actual experience in the woods, a less perfect outline of the trail will be found sufficient to tell the wild cat from the wild dog.

In snow five inches or more deep the lynx makes, as a rule, quite a drag with his feet, much more so than either fox or coyote, which latter disturbs the snow only near the individual tracks. On good tracking ground, or in soft snow, the nail marks are sometimes visible, but never prominent like those of the fox or coyote.

THE DOMESTIC CAT

THE track and trail of the house cat—(if it were only a house cat nothing would be said about it here)—is too well known to need description. If it is found anywhere in hunting grounds, parks, etc., the finder will confer a benefit on lovers of nature and its feathered denizens if he, where possible, will set a trap baited with fish (herring), or cheese; or if there is a chance to fill the "varmint's" anatomy with pellets from a shotgun or a .22 rifle, or to cut it in two with a big rifle bullet, he should never fail to do so. It may seem a waste of powder and lead, but it is not, for in my opinion there is no more harmful creature a-foot or a-wing than the domestic cat outdoors.

It would be impossible to estimate the amount of damage they do by killing songsters which nature intended to check insect pests. As far as the sportsman is concerned, a single cat will often deprive him of his shooting in given localities, for, if it has once found the location of a bevy of quail, grouse or other game birds, it will not stop until the last one of the family is killed.

Wild predatory animals generally restrict their raids to the hours of the night; a domestic cat will prowl and kill at any hour during the twenty-four. Some specimens attack even deer fawns and other game of like size.

A cat shrinks from nothing in its lust for killing—not even from water—and I remember seeing a big tom-cat rob a pond in a city park of its goldfish. Unluckily for the marauder I had a gun with me.

Anyone interested in shooting should keep a lookout for cat tracks in the woods during the summer and autumn, and do his best to let them show no more.

THE WOLF

THERE is perhaps no other animal about which more disagreeable things are said and written than the wolf, yet the writer, though recognizing its bad points, would dislike to have it become extinct. Its howl is inseparably associated with many of my pleasantest recollections, and the butte-fringed prairies and rugged Bad Lands would have decidedly less charm without it for one who has learned to love that so-called " God-forsaken country."

Except under unusually severe weather conditions, wolves generally kill only the weakest of range stock and big game animals, and I doubt if their so-called depredations in this respect are anything but a benefit to the survivors, as weaklings among any species of animals are always inimical to the general health and condition of the respective variety. The wolf in this regard does only what the sensible warden of a well-conducted game preserve does; *i. e.*, weeds out

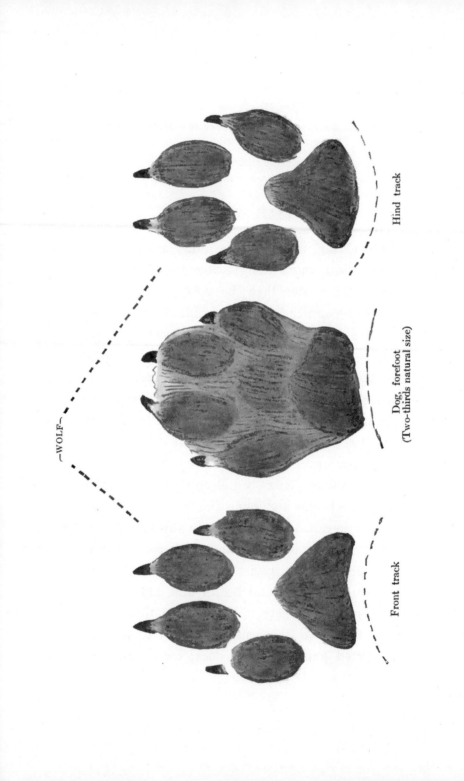

Hind track

Dog, forefoot
(Two-thirds natural size)

Front track

WOLF

undesirable specimens. In Yellowstone Park, for example, since the cougars there are systematically hunted with hounds, wolves and coyotes ought to be protected to a certain extent or else the result will undoubtedly be a general degeneration among the game animals in that region.

Before the warfare against lions was started, there were already many scabby elks in that great preserve, and if the slaughter of scavengers is kept up indiscriminately—well, a reasonable person can only await results with misgivings. Nature always works out her course best if left alone, and I believe that in the case of the Yellowstone Park the Nation in the course of time will be willing to pay ten times the amount it now pays for their extermination to have the " varmints " alive in that great preserve. Where weaklings are not abundant, game animals naturally suffer from an abundance of wolves, and where the stock-raiser has enough sense to dispose of sick or weak stock himself, Old Gray has no business.

In hunting wolves the quickest results are obtained in calling by imitating the cries of a jack-

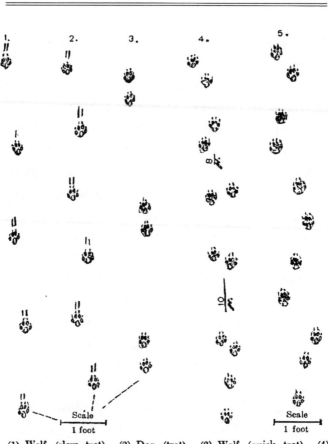

(1) Wolf (slow trot). (2) Dog (trot). (3) Wolf (quick trot). (4) Wolf (gallop). (5) Dog walking slowly; a motion never seen in the wolf trail.

rabbit. Wolves evidently think one of their tribe has caught a bunny, and, as Wildenbruch fittingly says: " Each and everyone would eat

112

him." This trait is shared by most other marauders. The wolf is a poor runner, and is easily run down with the aid of an ordinary horse in open country.

The surest and most effective way apart from calling, is by trapping, which is the most extensively practiced, and he who says that trapping is not great sport has surely never tried to outwit an old wolf. I always measure sport by the amount of skill required.

The keeper of a game preserve, who is not acquainted with the use of traps and other devices designed to decrease predatory animals, will never succeed in showing first-class results to the owner or owners so far as abundance of game is concerned; and what holds good in the case of the shooting-preserves holds good also for the open hunting grounds.

The track of an old full-grown wolf, although similar to that of a dog, differs from the latter, inasmuch as it shows that the foot is less fleshy, the soles of the various toes appearing more sharply divided than in the dog's track. The latter has a comparatively big foot. but also a soft foot which, being plainly visible in the ordinary gait, becomes much more apparent where the animal adopts a quicker motion. The toes are then spread out to an extent never found in the wolf, except when the latter is running very fast, and consequently the nail marks of the two middle toes of the dog are about twice as far apart as those of his wild relative. A wolf trail shows the individual tracks ordinarily about eighteen inches apart, while the dog, making the same size or a slightly bigger track, steps at the same gait less than fourteen inches; and if, in trotting, he should equal the length of wolf-steps, the spread of the middle toes makes his tracks easily recognizable. A good-stepping dog steps about as near the center line as the wolf, but as his steps are shorter, they appear more out of line to the eye. This is an optical illusion, but it serves the tracker's purpose.

A young wolf, say less than one year old, has as soft a foot as a dog's. However, as young wolves go mostly in packs, following the trail will generally reveal the identity of the animal. Usually wolves do not track continuously, one animal investigating here and another there, while the main trail leads on. Dogs, two or more, show no clear-cut single trail even for so short a space as ten feet, while a number of wolves often travel several hundred yards with the trail showing as though only one animal had made it. If one sees a wolf trail, and without following it concludes that it was made by a single specimen, he is liable to make the same mistake " Liver-eating " Johnson made with a bunch of horse-stealing Indians. He was stopping with a friend, Eugene Irvin, also an old Indian fighter, and one morning noticed about fifty horse-tracks, of which he concluded only about half-a-dozen were made by horses mounted by redskins. Instead of following out on the prairies and deciding there from the comparative absence of dust in the tracks—a rider is not mixed up with the herd he is driving, and consequently in his mount's tracks less dust is to be found—he hurried back to induce Irvin to join him in the pursuit of the Indians. Now that old scout was not as eager for the horses as " Liver-eating," and not at all for a fight, but for old friendship's sake said he would come along if a couple more fellows could be found, which, by the way, he did not believe possible, for the country was not settled then as it is now. But it happened that two men did come along just at that moment, and Johnson soon convinced them that profitable business was ahead if they joined in the pursuit. So the four went, taking a straight cut toward Horsethief, a section of the country southeast of the Big Snowy Mountains, where they thought the Indians would make a halt.

About three o'clock that afternoon they overtook the " Reds," but found to their chagrin that a dozen bucks were ready to give battle, while still four or five were left to attend to the stolen horses, and as neither Johnson nor any of his companions were burning for a fight, in which there was no promise of getting anything but bullet holes, Johnson decided that he would rather go home without the horses.

In the Bull Mountains a hunter followed a wolf trail into a ravine from which there was no escape for the "varmint" except past him, and he was promptly attacked by a half-dozen wolves. He killed four after a hard fight, but he was pretty well chewed up at the finish. Of course he had expected to find only one in the gulch.

As a rule the wolf is not anxious to fight, although not so cowardly as most other animals— the cougar for example—yet I have seen a single specimen follow a hunter, a boy of twelve years, but the best rifle shot I ever met, about two miles. I was with him, and waited for that wolf until he was within twenty yards, when I allowed the boy to fire. His nerves were evidently too much shaken, for he missed his first wolf—nevertheless he got his pelt.

The locating of dens, as explained in the discussion of the cougar, is also applicable to wolves.

THE COYOTE

WHAT has been said in regard to the wolf and dog track, is applicable also to the track and trail of the prairie wolf, but as the latter is small there always exists the possibility that its track will be mistaken for that of the fox. Where the locality gives no clue to the identity of the maker of the trail, the tracker has no distinguishing feature whatever from which to form his judgment, since a big red fox makes as big a track as a small coyote. The writer, after hunting foxes for many years, followed what he took for fox trails quite frequently in a certain section of the country, until he discovered that there was no fox within a couple of hundred miles of the place. A big coyote, of course, makes a larger track than a fox, but here all difference stops. For comparison's sake the track and trail of the *average* coyote and of the *average* fox are shown.

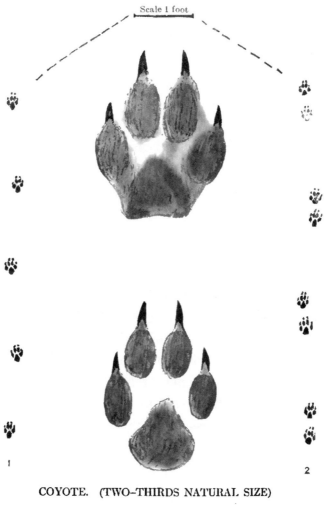

Scale 1 foot

1

2

COYOTE. (TWO–THIRDS NATURAL SIZE)

(1) Ordinary trot. (2) Fast trot.

The hunting methods are the same as for the gray wolf. Where the latter, however, is looking for the living, the coyote is watching for the dead, and he rather deserves to be called the hyena of the Western Hemisphere than prairie wolf, for his main diet is carrion. His addiction to carrion can be made of use to the hunter, in locating big game which has been unfortunately " shot to the woods," and of which he desires to secure at least the antlered or horned head.

In locating missing persons, who are supposed to have met with a fatal accident or worse, the trail of the coyote could be employed to advantage—and undoubtedly will be, if it is once a matter of general knowledge that the prairie wolf will always visit the immediate vicinity of the remains of a hidden or buried human body, and sound its dismal howl over them every time it happens to pass through that part of the country.

THE FOX

THERE is very little to add to what has been said about the fox track in the chapter on the coyote. When galloping, the fox's trail shows many variations not found in that of any other animal, but as the sinful fellow generally leaps only when he undertakes a chase, or is chased himself, the features in the running trail are practically of little or no consequence to the tracker. It is hardly possible to confound a fox trail with that of a very small dog—only in that the latter has a foot as small as the average fox—on account of the glaring dissimilarity in the length of the individual steps, which is much more apparent than between the wolf and big dog. The writer, at the tender age of seven, mistook once a very small dog's trail for that of a fox, but after his father pointed out the above feature, he never afterwards made such a mistake.

FOX. (TWO–THIRDS NATURAL SIZE)

Front and hind track. (1) Ordinary gait; the shaded part shows drag of brush. (2) Running.

When no individual track is visible, as is the case in dry snow, the blurry mark of the fox brush which is frequently seen at intervals in the trail settles any existing doubt. Some foxes, as well as wolves and coyotes, drag their feet to the same extent as does a dog that walks badly, and because of this the tracker may disregard as immaterial the prominence or absence of the drag made by the toenails.

Hunting foxes with hounds is undoubtedly the most popular method.

Calling him like the wolf and coyote yields good results for the still-hunter, but of all methods I prefer to shoot them during the rutting season, which occurs in January. The rutting season of coyotes is during February, and that of wolves from January 1st until April, approximately speaking. I have seen wolves "run" as early as December 28th, and have killed pups about two weeks old after the middle of June.

It is on snowy, blustering days that, in the depth of the woods, the fox is holding high carnival, and his and her tracks run in all directions.

Watching where the trails are most numerous soon furnishes work for the gun and trophies for the hunter, for on such occasions the fox seems to have lost the senses of sight and smell which at other times are so well developed. It is a singular fact that they always run the most during the worst weather. In driving it is impossible to tell where a wolf or coyote will leave a certain thicket, beyond that it will not leave it where it entered; but a fox is always the sure victim of the hunter if he knows the fox path, for like the bear or old boar, he and every one of his tribe will always leave a thicket at the same point.

In calling, an old fox, like a wolf, comes stealthily, while a young one, like a coyote, will generally be in a hurry to get there.

WHAT TRACKING MEANS, AND SOME HUNTING METHODS

BY the term "tracking" we usually understand the following of a trail, but if a hunter attempts to get a shot at his quarry solely by this means he has to depend on good luck or physical endurance. The cougar is, in my opinion, the most perfect tracker and most successful still-hunter; he tracks, but he does not follow the trail like a pack of wolves or dogs; he uses it only as a guide, following it for an occasional fifty or one hundred yards, which is to my mind the proper method for the human hunter.

Tracking also means the ascertaining of the preferred stand of certain animals. If, for example, the rutting place of the biggest elk in a district is located by comparison of various tracks, and the bull is shot later by waiting for, or stalking him at his favorite place, he undoubtedly falls a victim to tracking. Again, a track of a big bull moose is seen, and though it is too old to warrant expectations of finding the animal still in the locality, it is followed and determines where the bull made his resting-place. When, weeks later, perhaps, the fresh trail of the same bull is seen and again the previously preferred hillside, or another specific part of the woods is hunted over carefully without attention to the trail, but with all consideration for wind-direction and lay of country, and a fair shot is obtained, can it be doubted that tracking was responsible for the downfall of this monarch of the woods? If so, let the doubter once follow a moose track straight and try to get an easy shot: he will probably change his mind. The locating of game, sometimes weeks in advance of the time when the shooting is to be done, is not by any means the least feature in the art of tracking. To reduce, if possible, the annual slaughter of men by careless hunters, it may not be amiss to discuss certain hunting methods which have given me the most satisfaction, and which obviate the possibility of being fired at by mistake.

126

Stalking along in grown-up timber and other open places, the sportsman will run across the trails of all the animals which have moved in the district he covers, and, having decided which trail he wishes to follow, he keeps on in the direction it leads. If it enters a thicket, a circuitous route —under wind—will lead him to where the animal has passed out, or show him that it is "fast," *i. e.*, in the thicket. If the former, he, of course, has to pursue the same tactics until the game is located. The rest is generally easy enough, and that without entering any thicket, where, as we all know, it usually happens that hunters are mistaken for deer.

Many hunters in relating their experiences tell us how careful they were to hunt against the wind, to approach their game. While it is well enough to have the wind against one if the game is in sight or driven toward one, I consider it more judicious to make the wind serve me. Having located an animal in a thicket, I select a stump or some other elevation to windward which allows the widest possible view, and simply wait long enough to allow the wind to inform my quarry of my presence. It will not require long for the game to take the hint and get up—often affording a shot by this means alone—to leave the premises. Very few are the instances that an old buck goes straight away and gives me no chance to see him, because in that case he would have to cross my trail, and to do that the wind, or rather my scent, does not frighten him enough; and if he goes out at the side which is untainted by any scent of man, he is usually my meat—if he is up to my standard. If the thicket is too big, the smoke of a pipe will often do wonders. The biggest buck I ever shot, became my victim through the assistance of a smudge—the thicket in that instance being about ten acres in extent. The diagram (p. 130) will illustrate the method better than words could. I have used it with success on many animals, and even on a wounded bear.

During snowless times no one can know with certainty if a deer is in a certain thicket, and the method has to be employed at random where there are enough signs to make it likely that a buck is near.

In hunting against the wind in open forests more game is passed than many hunters would suppose. The animals see the man, note that he will pass them, and hide by getting as near to the ground as possible. If they scent him after he has passed, they evidently realize that the danger is over, though some, mostly the younger, inexperienced animals, then sneak off. Where game is very wild it is often in such localities as I have mentioned only possible to approach them *with the wind* by outdistancing the latter, because a big game animal at rest depends on its nose to save it from danger in the direction from which the wind comes, and on its eyes to watch the side from which it can get no other warning.

Desirable game is often located on slopes, and can be shot from an opposite slope if only it can be made to move around slowly, the latter being important, as shots in such cases have usually to be fired at long distance, and the ability to hit running game at three hundred or four hundred yards is not possessed by everybody.

An imitation of the lamenting cry of a jack-rabbit serves me best in such cases, though it has often saved the game I was after, because it has attracted a wolf, or a cat; and I would rather kill one " varmint " than half a dozen bucks, which last can at best elude a man who knows how to track for but a limited length of time.

HUNTING WITH THE WIND

The stand is at 2 if the hunter is alone, and uses only his scent or pipe smoke to drive the deer out of the thicket. If a smudge is used for this purpose, as is necessary in big thickets, the stand is at 1, and if the hunter has a companion, one stands at 1, and the other at 2. A smudge should be made distant enough from the thicket —about at 3—to give the hunter time to go around, and take his stand at 1.

The sketch of leaps of wounded animals apply to all of our hoofed game except bighorn sheep. In any case, where one of them has been fired at, the trail should be followed for at least two hundred yards, as often an animal that goes away with the bounds of an apparently sound creature, will announce its distress through the placing of its feet, a sure indication to the tracker that he will be able to get his victim at the trail's end.

PART ONE

GROUP II

THE JACK-RABBIT

THE jack-rabbit is generally a resident of open country, though he may be found also in woodlands; and, in some parts of the country, when deep snow covers the lowlands, he retires to the fastnesses of the mountains, where, up to altitudes of eight thousand feet, he frequents the range of Bighorn.

He is unquestionably the delight of the hunter who desires to acquire efficiency in hitting moving objects with a rifle bullet.

His tracks, being the biggest of the rabbit tribe, cannot very well be mistaken for those of any other animal. On sandy or muddy places often only the imprint of the front part of the hind foot is seen; and on hard roads, plow furrows, etc., usually the mark of the toenails alone is visible. When the animal is feeding or moving along slowly, the whole imprints of the hind feet are left, while with increasing speed only the front parts of them touch the ground. The

135

JACK-RABBIT

forefeet rarely pair, and never if a jack-rabbit is running. If the long-eared fellow decides in the morning that it is time to retire for the day, he usually runs along a road, cattle-runway, or the like, returns in his own trail, and by a long

136

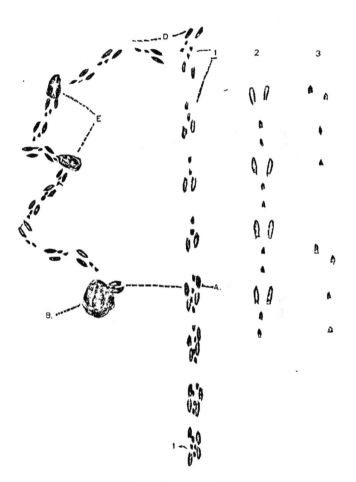

JACK RABBIT

(1) Morning trail (easy lope). (2) Moving slowly. (3) Speeding.
(A) Side-jump. (B) Day form. (E) Night forms. (B to D)
Morning trail and night trail (feeding).

side leap makes the trail seem to end. Where he lands, the four foot-marks are usually so close together that they can be almost covered with the hand. He may leap directly into his "form," or he may repeat the same maneuver several times; but one thing is certain, a jack which acts in this manner is never far from home. If pursued during the daytime, he employs the same tactics again and again to throw the pursuer off the trail. At feeding places slight forms are often observed, and to follow the trail leading from them means, as a rule, a tiring walk, as those forms indicate that the jack has spent the after-supper hours there.

I have hunted with men who blamed their dogs if they failed to catch a rabbit with a broken foreleg. They evidently did not consider that a broken foreleg is of very little consequence to the running efficiency of that kind of animal. One with an injured hind leg, however, can be run down easily.

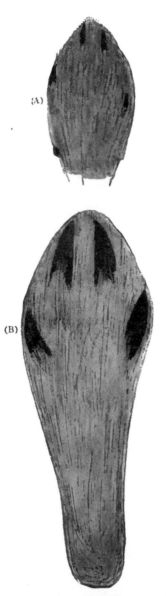

JACK RABBIT. (TWO–THIRDS NATURAL SIZE)
(A) Front foot.   (B) Hind foot.

THE VARYING HARE

THE Varying Hare, though scarcely half the size of the jack-rabbit, makes almost as large a track, and when he spreads his feet in passing over frozen snow his tracks are fully as large. The entire track picture, however, differs materially from that of the jack—the individual tracks stand much closer together, and the feet are usually paired. The hare makes many different track pictures, but he cannot long refrain from making the jump—shown slightly reduced in the illustration—and a following of the trail for a short distance will always dispel any existing doubt, even if the individual tracks are larger than those of a young jack-rabbit. There is a much greater likelihood of mistaking the varying hare's trail for that of the cottontail rabbit, with which it has many points of resemblance. Only the slenderness of the rabbit's foot serves as a distinguishing feature in the trail so long as

VARYING HARE

they are both unalarmed. If, however, they are put on the quick jump, the similarity of the two trails disappears.

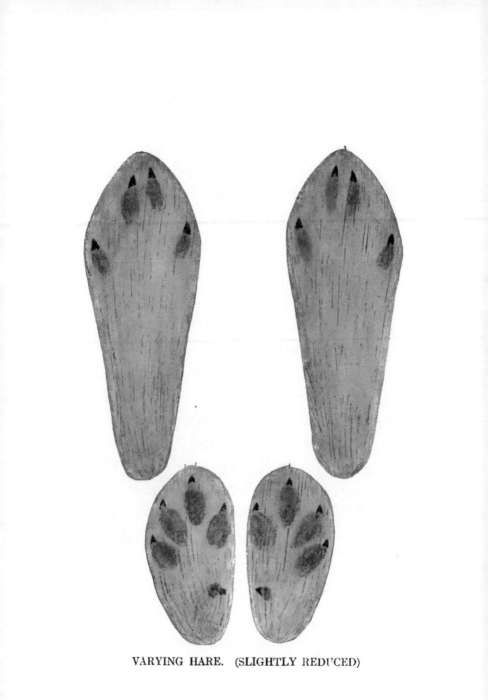

VARYING HARE. (SLIGHTLY REDUCED)

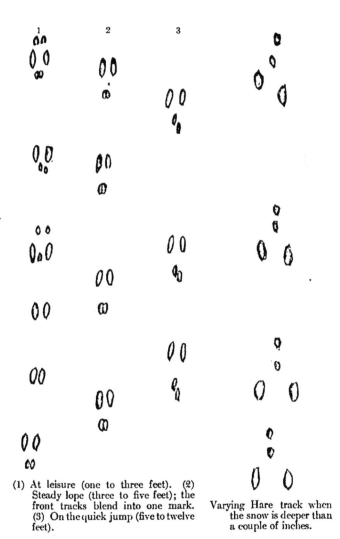

(1) At leisure (one to three feet). (2) Steady lope (three to five feet); the front tracks blend into one mark. (3) On the quick jump (five to twelve feet).

Varying Hare track when the snow is deeper than a couple of inches.

VARYING HARE TRACKS

THE COTTONTAIL RABBIT

A S can be easily seen from a comparison of
the life-size track picture of the varying
hare and cottontail—drawn from tracks
made under the same tracking conditions, *i. e.*, on
ground covered by about two inches of snow, and
while the animals were running at approximately
the same speed—the tracks of the cottontail, besides being much more slender than those of the
hare, are also more pencil-shaped at the point of
the toes. The toes are but faintly indicated, and
the toenails practically indiscernible, while in the
case of the hare both are plainly visible; in fact,
the imprint of the toenails is a prominent feature
in the track of the hare. In every case where any
doubt exists in regard to the tracks of the two
small varieties, this alone is sufficient to settle it;
as the toe marks are more prominent in the
front track, its appearance alone is sufficient for
the trailer to form a correct conclusion. Except
when jumping with the hind feet into the

front tracks two individual tracks
of the cottontail never blend into
one mark on account of the slenderness of the feet. The jump
picture of both the small rabbits
in dry snow sometimes appears
very much like that of the marten; but by following the trail for
a short distance one will always
dispel any doubt.

In illustrated articles the writer
has seen drawings and photo-
graphs of tracks and trails
claimed to have been made by the
New England cottontail which
looked exactly like those made by
the varying hare. If there was
no mistake in identification, the
Western cottontail, which the illustrations represent, evidently
makes tracks entirely different
from those of the Eastern variety. There is every reason to believe, however, that the track of

Cottontail Rabbit Tracks—(1) At leisure. (2) In a hurry.

145

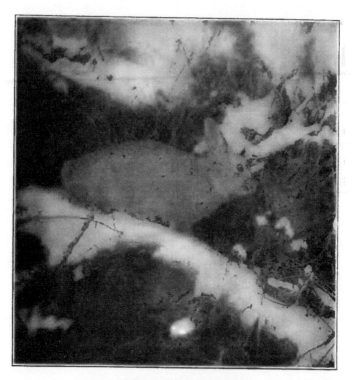

COTTON TAIL RABBIT

the same type of rabbit is the same in every part of the country.

While the pursuit of big game is exciting sport at times, hunting rabbits is always attended with soul-satisfying fun. A famous occupant of the White House found recreation and pleas-

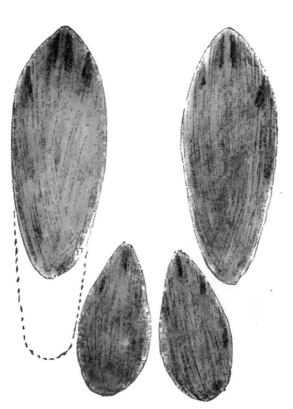

COTTONTAIL RABBIT

The dotted line shows the real length of foot.

ure in it, and I believe that few hunters who ever entered into the true spirit of the sport have failed to obtain a great deal of pleasure and healthful exercise.

147

THE SQUIRREL

THE squirrel practically always pairs its feet when on the ground. Like the other members of Group II its hind feet are much larger than the forefeet, and, as in the track-picture, are always planted ahead of the latter. The hind feet point outward, so that even by imperfect imprints, it may readily be seen in which direction the trail leads. As there is no other track known to the writer which could be confused with the squirrel's, it is not necessary to describe it; the illustration serves every purpose. Where the remains of the feast of a " varmint " are left in the woods—meat, entrails, or bones—squirrel tracks are found in great numbers, and the tyro is liable to take them for those of other animals. Ordinarily a careful look is sufficient to disillusion him, both as to the identity of the tracks and the diet of the squirrel.

Besides tracks, the squirrel leaves other signs which betray its presence in the woods—heaps of

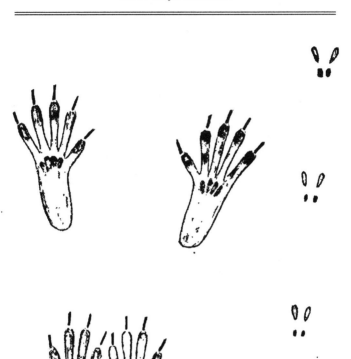

SQUIRREL. (ABOUT TWO–THIRDS NATURAL SIZE)

cone chips near stumps and other elevations, or strewn under trees one may find twigs from which buds have been eaten. Sometimes the cries of birds whose nests the squirrel may be robbing of eggs or young, will betray his presence. It is an entertaining pastime to hunt squirrels with a small-caliber rifle.

The writer considers the squirrel one of the most injurious creatures of our woods, and believes that in hunting him it is better to use some other weapon than the noisy shotgun.

PART ONE

GROUP III

THE MARTEN AND THE BLACK-FOOTED FERRET

THOUGH their habitat is entirely different, these two animals make very similar tracks and trails, so they are properly treated of in the same division.

While the marten is a resident of the woods, the black-footed ferret never leaves the open prairie, where it lives in abandoned prairie-dog holes, usually leaving its hole every second night, unless it happens to kill a rabbit. It is the most relentless enemy of the rabbit, and lives almost exclusively on its flesh.

The track of the black-footed ferret is about the size of a small marten's, but in soft snow the soles of the toes show more prominently than those of the latter, whose strongly haired feet usually cause the sole marks to appear rather indistinct.

Sometimes the trail of the marten looks like that of the cottontail, but if followed for a short distance it always assumes again the form of a

Marten track (one-third natural size), showing the four foot marks (not the usual jump, see trails). The black-footed ferret makes a slightly smaller track and shows not quite so much hair.

parallel trapeze, the evidence of the usual marten motion to which the ferret adheres at all times except in the pursuit of prey.

There is no reason for mistaking one for the other, because, as aforesaid, they do not inhabit the same locality; but if one does not know of the existence of the wild ferret, then, of course,

154

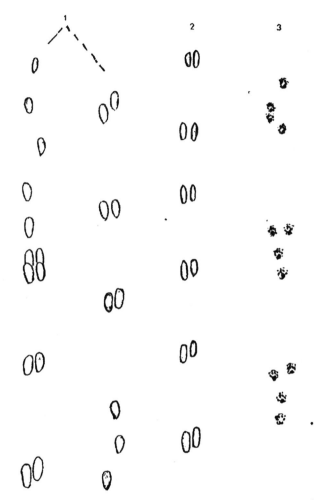

(1) Marten tracks. The lower part of the left-hand drawing shows the usual marten motion, namely, the jump. The upper part of the same drawing shows the walk, which is always only for a short distance. (2) The black-footed ferret always pairs its feet and never walks. (3) Running.

one might track a supposed marten on the prairie—as did the writer when he first came West—where that animal never has been found.

Tracking marten and shooting them is as successful a method as trapping them.

If ferrets are tracked and their skin is wanted whole, a trap not smaller than a No. 4 should be set at the entrance of the hole, as the pretty "varmint" mutilates himself if trapped and not soon killed. If a ferret runs a rabbit into a hole he may not leave it for two or three weeks, otherwise, as stated, the ferret usually travels forth every second night.

THE OTTER

IT can be seen from the accompanying illustration of front and hind tracks that the footmarks of the otter are rather unusually round; and on hard ground, which allows but a slight impression, the almost circular standing imprints of toes and heel show plainly. If the individual tracks are invisible in dry snow, the form of the trail, together with the drag made at intervals by the long tail of the otter, obviates any doubt as to what animal has made the trail.

The otter has a habit of leaving the streams along which he lives, or which he visits, at regular places, and makes what are called slides near which parts of fish are frequently scattered. Excrements containing fish bones found on boulders and promontories in the rivers are unmistakable otter signs that betray his presence, even if no tracks or slides are seen along the banks of the stream.

157

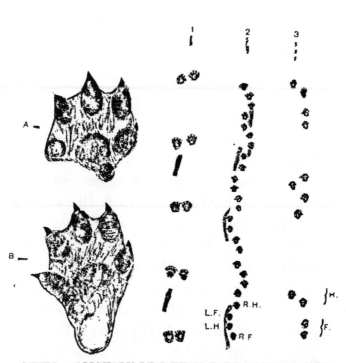

OTTER. (SLIGHTLY LESS THAN HALF NATURAL SIZE)

(A) Right forefoot track. (B) Right hind-foot track. (1) Jumping. (2) Walking. (3) Running. The shaded line shows the drag of the tail.

The otter is perhaps the greatest wanderer among the mammals, and may, therefore, frequently be found where he was supposed to be extinct; though if he visits a trout-stream or pond he usually makes his stay long enough to

158

deplete it to a greater extent than a host of fishermen would.

Where otter signs are seen along small streams or at favorable places along rivers, waiting for them with a shotgun during evenings and moonlight nights usually yields satisfactory results. If one is shot, and there is no danger of the current taking it away, it is well to keep quiet for a time, as they often fish in pairs, and the second frequently gives as good a chance for a shot as the first.

The whistling call of the otter can easily be imitated, and at big rivers on a clear night calling them is good sport. However, the sportsman must be patient, as the otter will answer immediately, but will take his own time in coming. On small streams it is well to post oneself as near as possible to the water, as otherwise the otter will pass unseen in the shadow of the bank.

Sometimes the otter travels for miles on land, and if daylight surprises him there he will hunt shelter for the day in any convenient hole. A trap set in it, and the entrance closed with a boulder is usually the easiest way to get his skin.

As the animal is especially destructive in trout streams the sportsman gunner will always do a great favor to the disciple of the rod when he closes the career of one of these four-footed poachers.

THE MINK

THE mink track presents some similarity to those of the marten and the black-footed ferret, but it is much smaller than that of the marten, and the toe-marks are even more prominent than those of the ferret, for which it might be mistaken at times if it were not that the form of the trails is different. The mink never travels for long distances without showing at least three tracks plainly in the jump-picture, while the ferret practically never does this. The track of the ferret is found near ice-bound streams only when it crosses them to reach other hunting-grounds, while the mink, being almost as skilful at catching fish as the otter, generally travels along a stream's course.

In destructiveness to small game the mink is perhaps only equaled by the domestic cat, which, in remote districts, he resembles in the habit of hunting at all hours of the day.

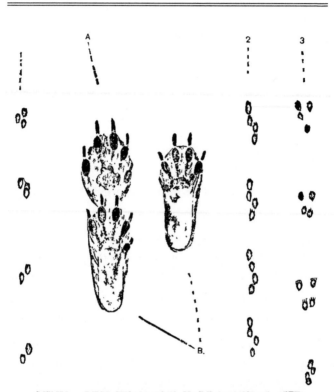

MINK. (LESS THAN ONE–HALF NATURAL SIZE)
(A) Left front-track. (B) Hind-tracks (a characteristic track picture).
(1) Ordinary jump. (2) Easy running. (3) Running.

Trapping is practically the only paying
method of hunting him. When he goes upstream he leaves the water below rapids and travels along its edge usually until he again reaches
quiet water. If a trap is placed in the interven-

162

MINK

ing space—the trail of the animal will show the trapper the best point—every mink in that vicinity may be caught without the trouble of baiting traps, which is a rather uncertain method where game and fish are plentiful.

THE ERMINE

ALL lovers of our feathered song-birds kill
the weasel at every opportunity, believing
it to be one of the deadliest enemies to bird-
life; and if sportsmen bear in mind that every
time it gets a chance the little marauder fastens
its teeth in the neck of a grouse or a rabbit, they
will undoubtedly show it no mercy. Considering, however, the number of injurious rodents it
kills, it is doubtful if this " little marten " is, on
the whole, more destructive than useful. Certainly it does no more harm than the absolutely
useless squirrel. I leave it to others to argue
whether it should be killed or spared. I do not
spare it in ruffed grouse cover and near home,
where I wish to give the birds absolute protection.

Its tracks and trail, with the exception of the
walk, which the weasel does not use where it could
be tracked, are exact miniatures of those of its
large relative, the marten, and are, judging from
personal observations, frequently mistaken for

those of other animals even by sportsmen of long standing. One will mistake its trail for that of the deer, another for that of a coyote, fox or lynx, and still another, under favorable tracking conditions, will confound its track with that of the mink or ferret. In loose snow, when its trail is likely to be mistaken for that of any of those mentioned, it should be considered that the jumps of the ermine constantly vary in length, while the individual tracks made by the other named animals usually stand a regular distance apart.

If the tracker follows an ermine's tracks which he takes to be those of a mink, he should soon discover that the animal has entered every hole and crevice along the trail, and that, judging by the number of tracks around them, it found rock piles, logs, brush heaps, etc., very interesting and attractive. Now, marten or mink investigate these things simply by passing over or through them—if they do not stop inside—but they never make regular paths around them as the ermine does. Besides this, the ermine makes a track hardly one-third as large as that of a small marten.

ERMINE TRACKS. (HIND FEET, LIFE SIZE)
(1) Ordinary jump.   (2) Running.

I have again and again pointed out the above features to men with whom I have hunted, yet, presumably on account of not being thrown on their own resources at the time, they seemingly paid little attention to them, for I observed that they repeated their mistakes just as soon as opportunity offered. The secret of successful trailing can be acquired only by the careful and observant.

The features of a track or trail, once they are thoroughly impressed on the mind, will always be remembered; and he who is too careless to take note of them, even when they are pointed out, has only himself to blame if he spends time—hours perhaps—in the pursuit of the trail of an animal he does not want.

PART ONE

GROUP IV

THE BEAVER

THE beaver was once distributed to a vast extent all over the globe, but is now found in comparatively few sections of the Old and New Worlds, and nowhere in great abundance. The state of Montana, which until recently had the largest number of them within its boundaries, joined, during 1907, those States

BEAVER

171

BEAVER

where this interesting animal is practically extinct, and the blackening " beaver stumps " along
its streams bear witness to the shame of the legis-
lative assembly of 1907, which left the beaver
without protection.   For the extermination of the
beaver in this State the wealthy classes, and not

172

BEAVER FEET (ONE-THIRD SIZE)

BEAVER. (ABOUT ONE–HALF NATURAL SIZE)
(A) Track of right hind foot. (B) Track of right forefoot.

the trappers, must bear the blame, for without the consent of the former the trapper could not even have decreased the number of them without endangering his own liberty.

Where the beaver *is* protected, he increases rapidly, and if hunted with a rifle, he affords as

174

BEAVER STUMP

THE BEAVER'S HOME

much excitement as any game that roams the woods.

Business instinct, as well as sportsmanship, should urge sportsmen to concerted action in order to preserve and increase the comparatively few beaver colonies now left on our continent.

The beaver's tracks most strikingly represent the fourth group of mammals in this treatise.

BEAVER TRAILS OR SLIDES

In the effort to support and steady the body adequately, the animal endeavors to plant its feet as near as possible under the center of its body, but its corpulency prevents, and the result is a track so ridiculous that it is laughable. The front tracks are covered with the hind feet, the third toe-nails of which reach the center line, and the heel of which stand, according to the size of the specimen which made the trail. from four to eight

BEAVER TRAIL
The third toe touches
the center line.

inches from it. The nails of the two inside toes of the hind feet are but to a limited extent visible as the web between the toes protrudes them. Where the beaver is scarce and much pursued, the imprint of a forefoot near the water's edge may be discovered occasionally here and there; in this case the prominence of the toe-nails is unmistakable. I may state here, that a front track at the water's edge is often the only sign which may be found along a stream where beavers have become very wary; they seem to be able to live on almost nothing—leaves, roots, etc.—for not a single cutting can be discovered in such cases. Where not sought extensively, the hunter seldom notes the tracks of this aquatic fur-bearer; cut willows or tree stumps are, if not a surer, at least a more easily distinguished indication of their presence, while on much-used slides the tracks could not be seen

178

anywhere. It has been the writer's experience that in every case in which he observed the building of a new house by one of these animals, the builder was invariably a' female providing for a happy family event.

THE BADGER

ON our continent there is no other animal which is responsible for so many broken necks and limbs as the badger. While in pursuit of his prey, he digs holes in the ground, which when grown over with weeds or grass, are almost certain death-traps for the unwary rider.

The man who enjoys riding after wolves or the fox considers the badger as a menace, and is never likely to look upon it with any degree of favor, notwithstanding its decided usefulness as a destroyer of undesirable rodents. I myself bit the dust of the prairie four times within a couple of months on account of this animal, though there was no further damage than a broken gunstock and sore limbs. I have since killed everyone of the tribe when a chance offered, though with some feeling of regret on account of their desirable features.

The track of the badger is striking from the prominence of the five-nail marks of the fore-

BADGER

feet and the twisted inward appearance of the hind track which usually stands squarely in the front track. Considering the size of the tracks, the step-marks stand close together—about seven inches—and, as in all animals of this group, to some extent off from the center line.

BADGER TRACKS; LEFT. (SLIGHTLY REDUCED)

It is readily tracked down, and when its hole is approached, the animal frequently exhibits its head as a target from its curiosity to see what is coming. If run into a hole, it will almost invariably reappear within a few minutes. If it offers no chance for a shot, a trap placed at the entrance and covered nicely generally brings about its destruction. If no trap is at hand it can be confined to its hole by tying a piece of paper or a rag to a stick and placing it not less than two feet from the entrance, which will prevent its leaving the hole for twenty-four hours or so. This is a surer method of keeping the animal a prisoner than blocking the entrance, and works satisfactorily also with other marauders that take to holes.

A fox can usually be held thus for several days, and by this ruse I have actually starved two of them to death. There was in each case three entrances, and but one trap at hand, which was in both instances uncovered by the prisoners during the first night.

As the ground was frozen hard, I did not wish to bother with setting the trap at another entrance, so I left things as they were, after covering the instrument again. But the foxes knew it was there all the same, and did not again try to leave their prison by that exit, and the other

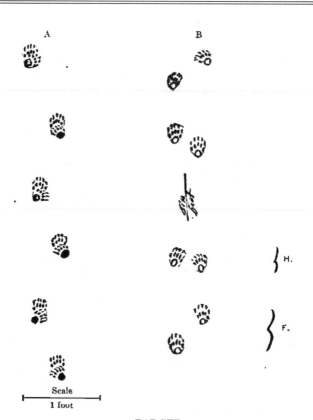

BADGER

(A) Walking. (B) Running.

entrances were guarded by that fearful specter of paper. Finally each one died about eight feet from the scarecrow—about five feet inside the hole, which was examined daily—one during

184

the nineteenth, and the other during the twenty-second day of their imprisonment. Had the ground not been frozen so hard as it was, the experiment would have been unsuccessful, as each of the foxes would of course have dug out at some other spot. The latter method of escape will be employed by the badger in every case where the trap is not properly covered.

THE PORCUPINE

IT may appear out of place to discuss this
creature which has no sportive quality whatever, but its trail is so conspicuous in snow
that it cannot be passed without being noticed,
and the tyro, attracted by the size of the tracks,
will in many instances follow it, thinking he is on
the trail of something else.

A short time ago I trailed a supposedly lost,
inexperienced hunting companion who had run
across the trail of a "bear," as he thought, and
followed and killed "Bruin," who happened to
be up a tree. When I caught up with the young
fellow, he was contemplating his broken gunstock, smashed in finishing the "varmint," but
proudly exhibited, to my great hilarity, the
"bear" which may have weighed about twenty
pounds, and whose fur consisted mainly of quills.

Before I got acquainted with the "pine-
porker," I tried in vain for a period of four

PORCUPINE

months to ascertain the identity of an animal whose tracks I frequently saw on a road. Only the marks of the soles were visible there, and none of the many men I asked knew that track, though they knew the animal which made it very

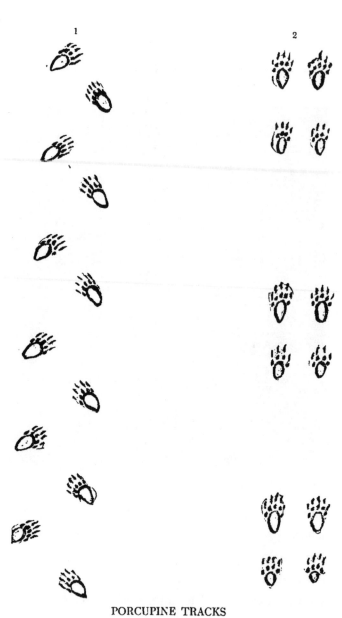

PORCUPINE TRACKS
(1) Walk. (2) Run.

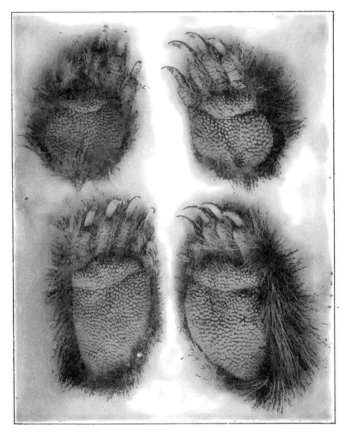

FEET OF THE PORCUPINE
Four toes on front and five toes on hind feet (about one-half natural size)

well, as developed later, when tracking conditions became so that I could follow the trail to its end.

189

SIGN OF THE PORCUPINE
(Bark eaten from the tree)

If conditions are half-favorable, the imprints of the toe-nails—four on the forefeet and five on the hind feet—are always visible.

If the snow is a few inches deep, the tracks stand in a trough-shaped trail because the animal's body almost touches the ground. The toes point inward, and almost touch the center line. In the snowless woods numerous small dead trees attract the attention of even those not interested in forestry. If these trees are examined they will reveal the mark of the porcupine, easily recognized by the partly eaten bark.

Along the streams of the Bad Lands the limbs of cottonwood trees are sometimes depleted of every vestige of bark, which loss ultimately causes the death of the trees. Where forests are cared for on an economical basis, the porcupine is certainly a proper subject for extermination.

Their meat is excellent if fried quickly in hot lard; roasted, or cooked slowly, it emits an odor repellent even to a hungry man.

191

THE SKUNK

THOUGH an inexcusable intruder in the chicken coop and where game birds are raised, the skunk is decidedly useful from the standpoint of the forester or of the farmer. In the writer's opinion, sportsmen if they encounter him in the woods should cease to kill the animal just because, it is " only a skunk "; others of the fraternity advance the " just because " argument if they are questioned why they " shoot " the nests of useful hornets. The skunk may rob a few birds' nests during the summer, but his main diet consists of larvæ and berries, and by destroying the former he is of inestimable value to the forests and fields near his residence.

I am thoroughly convinced that his introduction and absolute protection in localities where moths, butterflies and the like, in their undeveloped stage, have become a menace, would greatly help to solve the problem of rendering these pests harmless.

With every skunk we kill we interfere with the

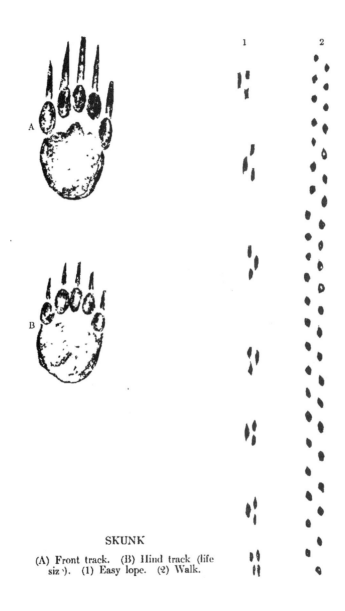

SKUNK

(A) Front track. (B) Hind track (life
siz·). (1) Easy lope. (2) Walk.

balance of nature, and the resulting deficit has finally to be met with the pocketbook by paying for artificial substitutes for nature, which if left alone would do the work much better.

In the summer woods it is not so much the skunk's tracks which tell of his presence and merits, as the numerous small holes in the ground, about a couple of inches deep, from which the animal procures the larvæ there awaiting the final stage of development.

The soles of the skunk's feet are similar to those of the badger, while their size about corresponds with that of the domestic cat; the toe-nails always show conspicuously under fair tracking conditions.

The individual tracks stand about half as far apart as do those of the domestic cat, and are always considerably out of line. Like the other members of this group, the skunk betrays himself by his trail; he is a slow animal, and presumably would not put on speed if he were capable of it, since, when foraging he is never in a hurry, and if molested it is usually the disturber who prefers to employ speed.

PART TWO

FEATHERED GAME

FEATHERED GAME

IT is out of the question to treat the signs and tracks of birds with the same thoroughness as those of mammals, because the tracks of several birds reproduce exactly those of domestic fowls, and those made by young birds of one kind may look like those of old birds of another variety.   A description of bird tracks will, however, be found interesting, and perhaps useful at certain times, especially by the inexperienced hunter.

The locality where a given track is seen is the main point to be considered.   Tame turkeys and domestic chickens do not, as a rule, venture great distances from the barnyard, so if tracks similar to theirs are seen far from human habitation, it is usually safe to conclude that wild birds made them.   In the case of waterfowls, however, even the consideration ·of the locality, under certain circumstances, does not exclude errors; so the hunter, if he sees tracks from which he might deduce the presence of these birds in his immediate locality, should employ his resources to find out for certain whether his deductions are correct or not. The descriptions are of necessity limited, and the reader should study the illustrations as the more important part of the matter.

UPLAND BIRDS

The Turkey

The tracks of this, the largest of game birds, differ in nowise from those of the domestic kind. In the woods—in wild turkey country—they usually indicate their presence by scratching up the ground cover in search of food, just as domestic fowls do under similar circumstances, and by their droppings. The latter are the more important as a means of identification.

Wild turkeys, when habitually or temporarily frequenting a given locality, have their favorite trees upon which they roost, and under these trees the droppings will be very plentiful. Some hunters wait at such roosting places during the evening or morning and get their game; sometimes the bird may have treed five hundred yards or more away, but the expert, who is not given to guesswork, makes it his purpose to ascertain all the turkey trees in a district, notes the easiest way to approach them, and then, during the early evening hours he will, from a convenient point, mark down the birds which he hears treeing. Then during the hour before daybreak he will go noiselessly as near as possible to a roosting tree which he knows harbors one or more turkeys, and after it is light enough to shoot he will experience little trouble in stalking as close as is necessary to get his bird.

The Sage Grouse

The track of the sage hen is about the size of that of a small domestic chicken, but the toes at their base are somewhat broader, giving the entire track a different aspect.

In the spring and autumn months the birds frequent sagebrush flats and hillsides, and during the early autumn they seek the vicinity of water, and there, if it were not that their toes are rather short in comparison with their broadness, the tracks might be mistaken for those of the pheasant in any place where that game bird has been introduced.

TURKEY. (LARGE DRAWING TWO–THIRDS
NATURAL SIZE)

(1) Walking.   (2) Strutting.

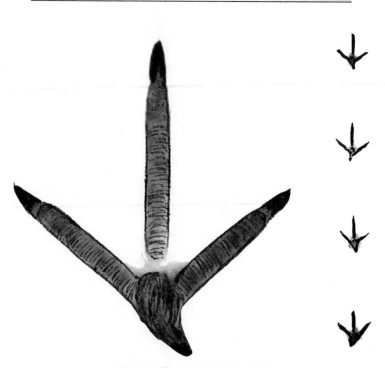

PHEASANT. (NATURAL SIZE)

Pheasant

The middle toe of the pheasant stands almost in a straight line in the trail, and this feature is the most striking one whereby to distinguish its track from the tracks of any of our native game birds.

202

Ruffed Grouse.   (Two-thirds natural size)   Blue Grouse.

Grouse

The members of this class, in which are included the various varieties of the ruffed grouse and those of the Spruce or Blue grouse, all spread their feet in similar fashion, and walk with the middle toes pointed inward to a considerable

203

RUFFED GROUSE

degree. Because of this similarity the size of the tracks and the length of steps are the only means by which to identify the particular species which made them. The ruffed grouse make the shortest steps and the smallest tracks.

BLUE GROUSE

The illustrations show the tracks and trail of a dusky grouse of ordinary size, and of an unusually big ruffed grouse cock.

The drawings were made under ideal tracking conditions; and only then is it possible to note the difference in the number of the knots of the

SHARP-TAILED GROUSE

middle toe. Though, as a general rule, the ruffed grouse usually frequents rather low country and the blue-grouse tribe is generally found on high grounds, the locality where a track is seen gives no sure indication of the species. The

206

Sharp-tailed Grouse.   (Two-thirds natural size)   Sage Grouse.

writer has frequently encountered the ruffed grouse at altitudes of over seven thousand feet, and the blue grouse lower down than he ever found the ruffed variety.

Prairie Chickens

From the prairie hen to the sharp-tailed grouse, they all belong to one order as far as their tracks are concerned. A prairie chicken does not spread the toes to the same extent as does the grouse of the woods, and the middle toes stand also somewhat straighter in the line of the trail. The tracks made by the sharp-tailed grouse are always of a rather blurred appearance because of the heavily feathered feet.

Quail

The size of the quail's track is about that of a domestic pigeon. A peculiarity of the track is that the mark of the hind toe stands comparatively far off from the track on account of its singular disproportion to the size of the foot.

In the pursuit of grouse, chickens, etc., the hunter usually notes tracks less than other signs. Foremost among the latter are the places where the birds take sand baths, where stray feathers will usually be found. Countless interwoven

QUAIL. (NATURAL SIZE)

small paths, leading everywhere and nowhere in grass and grain fields, are infallible signs that birds have fed there.

Woodcock

The neatest bird track seen in upland hunting is, in the writer's opinion, that of the woodcock. True, this fascinating Long-face has generally gone to warmer climes before winter sets in, but

209

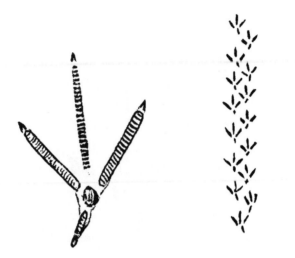

WOODCOCK. (NATURAL SIZE)

occasionally an early snowstorm catches him, and then his tracks are a striking feature near springy places in forests, or under dense trees that hold most of the snow aloft on their branches. The splendid imprints are as unmistakable among bird tracks as the tracks of the mountain sheep among big game, and as unforgettable if once seen.

210

WATERFOWLS

Swans, Geese, Ducks

The tracks of these aquatic game birds are so much alike that only the difference in size makes it possible to distinguish the species and varieties of ducks and geese; if they are of similar size they cannot possibly be told apart. Where the tracks are seen during cold weather at small open streams or springs, it is certain that the birds visit there at night, doubtlessly coming from a big stream or lake, perhaps many miles distant; by waiting for them at sundown royal sport can be obtained. During summer, on grassy places near water, young geese and ducks usually make numerous small paths, similar to those made by upland birds, but broader.

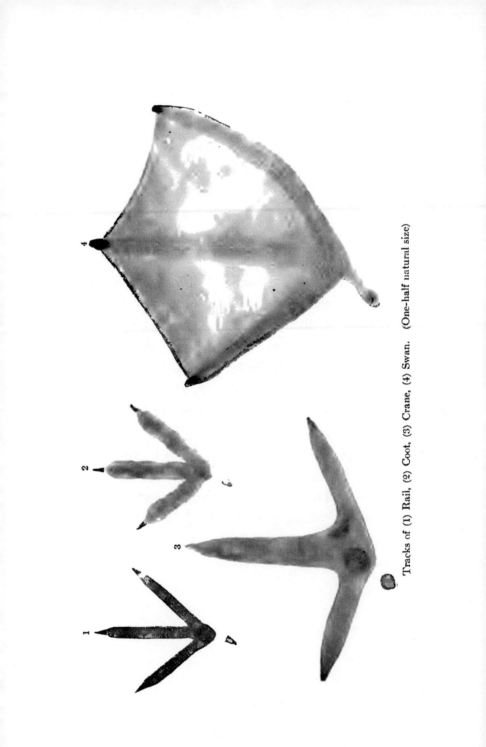

Tracks of (1) Rail, (2) Coot, (3) Crane, (4) Swan. (One-half natural size)

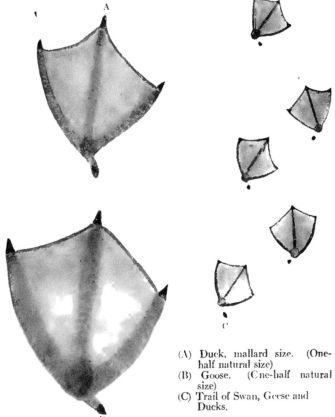
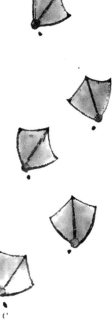

(A) Duck, mallard size. (One-
    half natural size)
(B) Goose. (One-half natural
    size)
(C) Trail of Swan, Geese and
    Ducks.

PREDATORY BIRDS

The Great Horned Owl

The great horned owl is of interest to the sportsman merely by reason of the depredations which some members of this tribe commit on small game. Where not forced by a scarcity of small game to subsist on mice, etc., this owl lives almost exclusively on rabbits and birds. The writer remembers an instance where one specimen killed every beaver kid and muskrat on a creek several miles along its course. The owl's tracks are very rarely seen, but from the undigested refuse which he ejects through his mouth (for he swallows all his prey, hair, bones, etc., when feeding) frequently found thickly strewn under his favorite roosting trees (usually densely branched), it can readily be ascertained what the light-shy fellow lives on, and if he proves to be an outlaw, his death will benefit the hunting ground.

Hawks

Notwithstanding claims to the contrary, all hawks, with the exception of the sparrow hawk, are injurious. Even the much-lauded marsh hawk in open districts lives exclusively on small birds, that is, at least, in the West. In timbered country, where he is too ungainly to catch winged prey, by force of necessity he has to subsist on small injurious rodents which he can catch in the open.

Whoever has observed with open eyes and an open mind the actions of hawks, knows that it will pay the sportsmen well to fill them with lead at every opportunity. Imitating their mating call—an easy matter—is the most satisfactory method of getting them within range, and it is also a very entertaining pastime during the close season. The hunter selects a good cover for himself in a locality which he knows or suspects to be infested by the pests, and sounds his *cac-cac-cac*—or, *kee-kee-kee-e-e*—dependent upon which variety of eagles or hawks he wishes to call, and if a hawk is within hearing, he is never long in coming.

215

SHARP-SHINNED HAWK

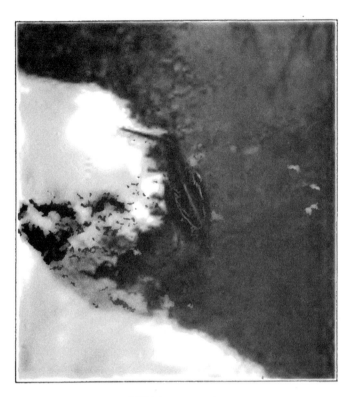

WILSON'S SNIPE

Various Birds

For the sake of comparison, and because also some of them are very interesting, results of my observations of the tracks of several birds not of the game class are herewith given.

217

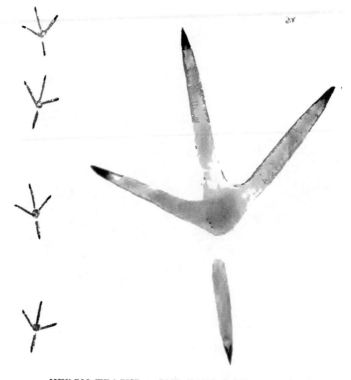

HERON TRACKS. (ONE-HALF NATURAL SIZE)

Bittern is the same form, but smaller. (The large drawing is of the right track.)

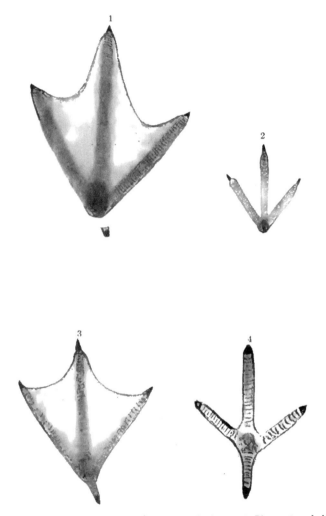

Tracks of (1) Flamingo (one-half natural size). (2) Plover (one-half natural size). (3) Gull (one-half natural size). (4) Dove (full size).

Notes and Drawings

Notes and Drawings

Notes and Drawings

Notes and Drawings

Notes and Drawings

Notes and Drawings

Notes and Drawings

Notes and Drawings

Notes and Drawings

Notes and Drawings